Preacher,
keep yourself
from idols

Derek Tidball

Preacher,
keep yourself
from idols

ivp

INTER-VARSITY PRESS
Norton Street, Nottingham NG7 3HR, England
Email: ivp@ivpbooks.com
Website: www.ivpbooks.com

First published 2011

British Library Cataloguing in Publication Data
A catalogue record for this book is available from the British Library.

ISBN: 978-1-84474-496-1

Set in Adobe Garamond 12.5/16pt
Typeset in Great Britain by CRB Associates, Potterhanworth, Lincolnshire
Printed and bound in Great Britain by Ashford Colour Press Ltd, Gosport, Hampshire

Inter-Varsity Press publishes Christian books that are true to the Bible and that communicate the gospel, develop discipleship and strengthen the church for its mission in the world.

Inter-Varsity Press is closely linked with the Universities and Colleges Christian Fellowship, a student movement connecting Christian Unions in universities and colleges throughout Great Britain, and a member movement of the International Fellowship of Evangelical Students. Website: www.uccf.org.uk.

Dedicated to David Coffey
Preacher, Christian statesman,
colleague and friend

CONTENTS

The idols of the ministry

ABBREVIATIONS

BST	The Bible Speaks Today series
DNTT	*Dictionary of New Testament Theology*
JSNTS	*Journal for the Study of the New Testament Supplement*
JSSR	*Journal for the Scientific Study of Religion*
NPNF	Nicene and Post-Nicene Fathers of the Christian Church
PNTC	Pillar New Testament Commentary
SNTS	Society for New Testament Studies
WBC	Word Biblical Commentary

PREFACE

Books on preaching are legion and I am loath to add to them. As will be evident to anyone who reads this book, I am indebted to many who have written in this area, and not least to some of the more classic volumes by Phillips Brooks, C. H. Spurgeon and P. T. Forsyth which, despite their age, still have much to say to preachers today. So, why another book?

Gordon-Conwell Theological Seminary invited me to deliver the Ockenga Lectures on Preaching in March 2010. It was a privilege but a daunting task, not only because of the name with whom the lectures were associated, but also because of the great contributions GCTS has made and continues to make to homiletics. And, since the lectures were annual, what more could be said which others had not already said? As I reflected on my theme, however, I decided to approach my subject obliquely and reflect on some of the temptations preachers face as a way into addressing some contemporary issues and doing so positively. Knowing my own heart, I am aware that preachers are subject to the temptations of idolatry as much as any other Christian, even if the idols that seduce them are peculiar to their calling. Hence, we preachers need to be alert to and equally unyielding to the amorous overture of idols. These reflections may have some wider use beyond the audience who originally gathered to hear them.

The fellowship of the community at Gordon-Conwell is always enriching and I am especially grateful to Drs David Horn, Scott Gibson, Jeffery Arthur and Ken Swetland who welcomed and entertained Dianne and me on our visit. My debts to others are wide and include friends with whom I have discussed various parts of these lectures and, once more, Jenny Aston at London School of Theology, and my family. The book is dedicated to David Coffey, former General Secretary of the Baptist Union of Great Britain and President of the Baptist World Alliance. David has shared many significant occasions with my wife and me and has been a valued colleague in ministry who has demonstrated enviable (I know that is one of the temptations for preachers!) gifts of preaching.

Derek Tidball
Leicester
May 2010

INTRODUCTION: THE NATURE OF IDOLATRY

Preachers. Idols. Surely not! The words surely do not belong together any more than a snowman belongs in a sauna. Or do they?

The apostle John ends his first letter with the plea, 'Dear children, keep yourselves from idols' (1 John 5:21). It seems a curious missile to launch as his parting shot and initially does not seem to be a very appropriate way of concluding his letter. He has not mentioned the subject of idolatry up to this point, so it inevitably raises questions as to why he makes it the subject of his final counsel.

The first question has to be what idols John has in mind.[1] Given his long association with Ephesus, where the Temple

---

1. See Stephen S. Smalley, *1, 2, 3 John*, WBC 51 (Waco: Word: 1984), pp. 309–310; and, more briefly, Colin G. Kruse, *The Letters of John*, PNTC (Grand Rapids: Eerdmans; Leicester: Apollos, 2000), p. 201.

of Diana was located, it would not be surprising if he had literal idols in his sights. Idols were omnipresent in the ancient world and none of the early Christians would have needed convincing of the daily importance of John's warning. They knew only too well the power of seduction that idols could exercise.

In context, however, John's missile seems to be directed at another target. The warning appears to stand in deliberate contrast to the verse before it, which speaks of Christians as 'in him who is true by being in his Son Jesus Christ. He is the true God and eternal life' (1 John 5:20). The implication is that Christian experience, as opposed to idol worship, is marked by truth rather than falsehood, authenticity rather than pretence, and life rather than death. So, instead of literal idols, John most probably had in mind the false teaching he has been denouncing in no uncertain terms throughout his letter, teaching that denied the real flesh-and-blood humanity of the incarnate and the risen Christ and therefore preached a false and inadequate Saviour.

That is how many have understood it down the centuries. Bede took it that way and wrote,

You who know the true God, in whom you have eternal life, must keep yourselves away from the teaching of the heretics which lead only to eternal death. In the manner of those who made idols in the place of God, the heretics have corrupted the glory of the incorruptible God by their wicked doctrines which bear the stamp of corruptible things.[2]

Then again, John might also have been picking up something else he had mentioned earlier. In 1 John 2:16 he urged his readers not to love the world, since it was composed of 'the cravings of sinful people, the lust of their eyes and their boasting about what they have and do'. The world is full of images which appeal to the eye and the psyche, and they easily create an appetite which they can never satisfy. Here, then, was another kind of idol to be avoided. What the world offered may have been powerfully seductive, but in reality it was a false phantom and a vacuous fancy. So John's admonition proves, in more ways than one, to be a very suitable conclusion to his letter and a necessary reminder to all of us to keep alert to the insidious temptations of all kinds of idols.

Idols come in all sorts of forms. In the Bible idolatry is a complex and varied concept even though it is transparently clear in its essence. At its heart it is 'anything that occupies the place of God'.[3] Classically, an idol was an image crafted by people's own hands and then foolishly bowed down to

---

2. Cited by Ben Witherington III, *Letters and Homilies for Hellenized Christians, Vol. 1, A Socio-Rhetorical Commentary on Titus, 1–2 Timothy and 1–3 John* (Downers Grove: IVP Academic; Nottingham: Apollos, 2006), p. 562.

3. B. F. Wescott, *The Epistles of John: The Greek Text with Notes* (Grand Rapids: Eerdmans, 1966), p. 197, cited in Smalley, *1, 2, 3 John*, p. 309.

in worship. It was this kind of idolatry that was not only explicitly forbidden in the Ten Commandments,[4] but was mocked mercilessly by the prophets.[5] Such idols still populate various parts of our world.[6]

Idolatry occurs just as often in the Western world where there is no literal image to be seen.[7] It can be an element of God's good creation, an aspect of leisure, or a philosophy or ideology that assumes an inflated place in our affections. Many idols are distortions of things which in themselves are good. But their importance becomes exaggerated and they become objects of worship, ends in themselves, instead of a means to the end of serving and glorifying God. Reinhold Niebuhr put this technically when he said that idolatry occurred when we 'make some contingent and relative vitality into the unconditional principle of meaning'.[8] When that happens, when anything assumes too much importance, however good it may be in itself, it threatens to supplant God and inevitably becomes destructive of our relationship with him. This form of idolatry is

---

4. Exod. 20:4–6; Deut. 5:8–10.

5. 1 Kgs 18:16–46; Isa. 46:1–13; Jer. 10:1–16.

6. On a visit to Cuba many years ago I learned that a regular aspect of pastoral work when families were converted to Christ was cleansing their houses of idols, which the pastor would then take home and burn.

7. While the so-called 'developed' world may shun literal images, certain places may become powerful symbols of idolatry, such as Wall Street being a powerful symbol of the idolatry of capitalism to which many bow down.

8. Reinhold Niebuhr, *The Nature and Destiny of Man*, Vol. 1 (London: J. Nisbet, 1941), p. 178.

more subtle than others. It can act like a cancer, growing silently inside us, all undetected until it is advanced and even too late to treat. Hence we need to be alert, as John knows.

Fallen human nature is fatally prone to idolatry, even when that fallen human nature is in the process of redemption, and even when it belongs to someone in a leadership position among God's people. It was not long after Israel had witnessed the miracle of the exodus that Aaron succumbed to popular pressure and built an idol – surely a salutary warning for us all.[9] Calvin was right when he insisted that 'the human mind is, so to speak, a perpetual forge (factory) of idols'.[10] While it is true that believers have dethroned idols and have bowed in service to the living God (1 Thess. 1:9), lifeless idols (paradoxically) continue to snap at their heels like energetic and untrained terriers. John was aware of the need to keep alert and kick them away before they nip us and draw blood.

While no preacher today would bow down to literal images, there are more subtle forms of idolatry that can prove to be temptations. Messengers of God are particularly vulnerable to the kind of idolatry that is a distortion of what is good. All Christian leaders are familiar with the way in which their service for God can become the end game of their lives, displacing God himself. Honesty would compel many of us to admit that at times 'the work' and

9. Exod. 32:1–35.
10. John Calvin, *Institutes of the Christian Religion*, 1.11.8.

'the ministry' are the reason for our existence. We find our identity in 'the service' we render, rather than in any real relationship with the living God. It is possible to continue to go through the motions of ministry, and even on the surface to be quite effective in ministry, long after the relationship has died.

Personally, I have found one of the most challenging prayers to pray (just in case God takes me seriously!) is that found in the Annual Methodist Covenant Service. It contains the words,

I am no longer my own, but yours.
Put me to what you will, rank me with whom you will;
Put me to doing, put me to suffering;
Let me be employed for you *or laid aside for you,*
exalted for you or brought low for you;
Let me be full, let me be empty;
Let me have all things, let me have nothing;
I freely and heartily yield all things to your pleasure and
    disposal . . . [11]

What is true of Christian life and ministry in general is true of preaching in particular, and John will, I believe, have sympathy with our taking his general warning to all Christians as a specific warning to preachers who can easily fall prey to the idols associated with their calling. We

11. Methodist Covenant Service, *Methodist Service Book* (London: Methodist Publishing House, 1984), p. 180, italics mine.

sometimes refer to them as 'occupational hazards', but that may be to treat them too lightly and excuse ourselves too easily. Idols are what they are.

In reviewing the idols to which preachers are particularly vulnerable, my aim is *not to condemn*, for the task is perilous enough, *but to alert* so that those factors which, although good in themselves, become idolatrous, deposing the living God from the throne which is rightly and exclusively his, can be avoided. My aim is not a negative one – the mere exposure of idols, but rather a positive one – the exposure of idols so that we may offer up our preaching as a worthy sacrifice to the one true living God.[12]

No preacher will succumb to the influence of all the idols I have identified. What proves a temptation for one will leave another untouched. But as ministry progresses we might well find ourselves vulnerable to idols that have never troubled us before. We are all likely to be at risk at some stage. Reviewing the whole inventory of idols, then, may serve as preventative medicine, prompting us to avoid temptations and be alert to vulnerabilities for which we are currently unprepared.

There are, of course, various ways in which 'the factory of idols' could be arranged, but for the sake of convenience I have chosen to organize them under four headings: namely, idols associated with the self, the age, the task and the ministry.

12.The comprehensive call of Rom. 12:1–2 must include our preaching.

THE IDOLS OF
THE SELF

1. THE IDOL OF THE PULPIT

Some idols lie very close to any preacher's heart. They have to do with the preacher's core identity and affect both personal and vocational self-understanding. The idols relate to the nature of the calling to be a preacher and the sort of people who respond to that calling.

Three such idols may be identified: the idol of the pulpit, the idol of authority (or power) and the idol of popularity.

To describe the pulpit as a potential idol is perhaps a surprising place to begin, especially as 'the pulpit' is being used not in the sense of a raised platform from which the preacher speaks, but as a synonym for preaching itself. The platform from which someone preaches may have symbolic significance. It can be a symbol for the status of the preacher which can corrupt his or her motives and become an end in itself. Its elevation above the congregation may suggest that the preacher is above the congregation in authority or holiness: famously 'six foot above contradiction'. Today, however, one is more likely to speak from a rickety and precarious makeshift platform shared with a group of musicians who have barely left the preacher enough room to stand. The reduction in elevation and the incursion of others into the space is symbolic either of the lessening authority of the preacher in some circles, or, in others, of a more 'innocent' accommodation to forms of communication that fit contemporary culture. But the pulpit as a platform is not our concern here.

Affirmations about preaching

The pulpit can easily become an idol because the activity it represents – that is, preaching – can become an end in itself. Preachers can become pulpiteers. This is not to say all preaching is idolatrous. Far from it. God has given teachers to his church who play a very significant part in proclaiming, applying and preserving the integrity of the gospel.[1] It remains an immense privilege to be called to be a preacher and I readily affirm its importance in the mind and ways of God. Astonishingly, God continues to use preachers as the medium through which he not only speaks but brings his creative, life-giving and transforming word to people's

---

1. e.g., 1 Cor. 12:28; Eph. 4:11; Col. 1:28; 1 Tim. 2:7. For an exposition of Paul as a teacher of the gospel, see Derek Tidball, *Ministry by the Book: New Testament Patterns for Pastoral Leadership* (Nottingham: Apollos; Downers Grove: IVP, 2008), pp. 127–145.

lives. I have no doubt about its significance or potential effectiveness. Our God is a God who from the very beginning spoke and his words made things happen. Down the centuries he has chosen preachers of one sort or another to continue this work of conveying his words and producing their desired effect.[2] As Sidney Greidanus puts it,

> Contemporary preaching of the gospel . . . is an indispensable link in the chain of God's redemptive activity which runs from Old Testament times to the last day (Matt. 24:14). God uses contemporary preaching to bring his salvation to people today, to build his church, to bring in his kingdom. In short, contemporary preaching is nothing less than a redemptive event.[3]

Whatever the qualifications, the trajectory that leads from Moses, through the Hebrew prophets and the apostles, and down through the centuries to the contemporary sermon forms a path which is connected and shows marked coherence, while at the same time it also demonstrates

---

2. My theology of preaching is very similar to Peter Adam, *Speaking God's Words: A Practical Theology of Preaching* (Leicester: IVP, 1996), pp. 15–56.

3. Sidney Greidanus, *The Modern Preacher and the Ancient Text: Interpreting and Preaching Biblical Literature* (Grand Rapids: Eerdmans; Leicester: IVP, 1988), p. 9. With him, I agree that this does not apply to all 'so-called' preaching, but to preaching that speaks the word of the Lord, and our only measurement for judging whether that is so or not is by the Bible.

change and development. Preaching is a significant instrument which God has used and continues to use under the direction of the Holy Spirit to communicate his word to those he has created. Consequently, preaching has always been a significant barometer of the health of the church over the centuries. P. T. Forsyth asserted its importance but was nonetheless probably correct when he began his lectures, entitled *Positive Preaching and the Modern Mind*, with the statement, 'It is, perhaps, an overbold beginning, but I will venture to say that with its preaching Christianity stands or falls.'[4] Indeed, perhaps such a claim is overstated and begins to hint at the way in which preaching may become idolatrous.

Preaching as idolatry

In spite of these positive affirmations about preaching, there are signs that preaching, and its contemporary form 'the sermon', is in danger of being idolized in some circles today. In recent days, the number of conferences, training courses, workshops, addresses and publications that celebrate 'the glory of preaching'[5] have greatly increased. In many of these the role of preaching – for which read 'the contemporary sermon' – is exalted and awarded the

---

4. P. T. Forsyth, *Positive Preaching and the Modern Mind* (London: Hodder and Stoughton, 1907), p. 3.

5. This is, I think, the unfortunate title of an otherwise excellent book by Darrell Johnson (Downers Grove: IVP, 2009).

status of being an essential and indispensible means by which the dying church is to be revived and a healthy church replenished. Other means of reviving the church are downgraded and other marks of a healthy church are recalculated so that preaching assumes the place of supreme importance.

Curiously, the number of such claims have increased almost in direct, inverse proportion to the decline of the importance of preaching in the popular mind,[6] and of criticisms of it within the church.[7] Those of a suspicious turn of mind might think that those who advocate the glory of preaching suffer from a severe case of cognitive dissonance.[8] Cognitive dissonance leads to our adopting strategies to ease the discomfort between knowing our position cannot really be sustained and our ongoing commitment to it and even advocacy of it anyway. Usually it is based on the mistaken understanding that the more

6. There is little evidence of its decline within the church. On the whole surveys show that it is greatly appreciated by those inside the church, while masses voluntarily attend conferences where preaching is central. See Mark Greene, 'Is anybody listening?', *Anvil* 14 (1997), pp. 283–294; and Ben Blackwell et al., *The View from the Pew* (Durham: Codec, 2009).

7. The most systematic (and flawed) critique is found in David Norrington, *To Preach or Not to Preach* (Carlisle: Paternoster, 1996).

8. Cognitive dissonance is based on the research of L. Festinger, H. Riecken and S. Schachter, *When Prophecy Fails* (San Francisco: Harper & Row, 1956), in which they explained why members of a cult who had prophesied the destruction of the world and whose prophecies had been disproved continued to be members. Vigorous proselytism often characterizes such groups.

we can persuade others to believe what we believe, the
more it must be true. It is a form of the old joke about
the preacher's sermon notes on which was written,
'Argument weak, shout louder!'

One example of this overblown status is found in the
work of the greatly and deservedly respected Martyn Lloyd-
Jones. In his lectures on preaching he argued that there was
'no substitute' for it.[9] Reviewing other forms of ministry,
he dismissed them as essentially relieving symptoms rather
than providing cures. He argued that personal counselling,
or a man who reads about salvation on his own, or one
who watches television and finds Christ, has missed out in
some way. The 'very atmosphere', he writes, 'of Christian
people meeting together to worship God and to listen to
the preaching of the Gospel' is part of the mystery God
uses to accomplish his purposes.[10] But, beneficial though
such a setting may be, this is surely a half-truth at best. It
certainly does not fit the sweep of biblical evidence. Stephen
before the Sanhedrin, the eunuch on the way home from
Jerusalem to Ethiopia, the Philippian jailer and the people
debating at Athens do not conform to this model and were
not subject to the sort of preaching Lloyd-Jones was
advocating. God is not as restricted in the way he works
as we frequently wish he were. God clearly has not read
our rulebooks.

---

9. 'No Substitute' is the title of the second chapter of Martyn Lloyd-Jones,
   Preaching and Preachers (London: Hodder and Stoughton, 1971).
10. ibid., p. 43.

Citing Ephesians 3:8–10 ('His intent was that now, *through the church*, the manifold wisdom of God should be made known to the rulers and authorities in the heavenly realms'), Lloyd-Jones argued, 'My whole contention is that it is the Church alone who can do this, *and it is the preacher therefore who alone can make it known*. He is set apart by the Church . . . to serve this particular function, to perform this particular task.'[11] In the wider context Paul had indeed been talking about his calling as an apostle, but he had then broadened his argument to include the church in its collective life as the means by which God would announce the gospel to the unseen powers of the universe. There is no legitimate reason for narrowing this role to 'the preacher alone'. God works through the church as a whole, through many different witnesses, not all of whom are preachers. The demonstration of its members' transformed lives, their exercise of love and their use of the varied gifts which make up the body are all used by God, not just the mouth! Through its ongoing life, the whole church proclaims the gospel.

Lesslie Newbigin was on much surer biblical ground when he wrote about mission, 'I am suggesting that the only answer, the only hermeneutic of the gospel is a congregation of men and women who believe and live by it.'[12] A congregation, note, not a preacher.

---

11. ibid., p. 29, italics mine.
12. Lesslie Newbigin, *The Gospel in a Pluralist Society* (London: SPCK, 1989), p. 226.

Some evangelicals have an almost sacramental view of the sermon and imply it is the exclusive, or near exclusive, means God uses to channel his grace today. They are in danger of displacing the biblical sacraments of baptism and the Lord's Supper by the sacrament of the word.[13] But this is surely to be questioned and potentially leads us in the direction of idolatry as easily as did some of the medieval and superstitious views of the Catholic mass.

Some contemporary talk about the sermon echoes Israel's trust in the temple that Jeremiah so roundly denounced in his 'Temple Sermon'.[14] Israel placed their trust in the erroneous belief that the mere existence of the temple in the heart of their community would give them security and exempt them from God's judgment. To trust in this, Jeremiah said, was to trust in 'deceptive words that are worthless' (Jer. 7:4, 8). To trust in the presence of fine and abundant preaching, as if that alone brings security and makes for spiritual health, is similarly to court disaster rather than the blessing of God. According to Jeremiah, it is not the chanting of mantras about the temple, but just and righteous living that brings security. So it is with preaching. It is not our devotion to the pulpit, nor the frequency with which we preach or taste sermons, but the practice of righteous and Christ-like

---

13. Dietrich Bonhoeffer termed it this in *Wordly Preaching*, ed. C. E. Fant (Nashville: Thomas Nelson, 1975), p. 111.

14. Jer. 7:1–18.

lives that counts. Anything else is no more than empty words.

Preaching and the modern sermon

Part of the problem with those who advocate 'the glory of preaching' lies in the neat equation that is often made between God as a communicator and the form of the contemporary sermon. The equation is often an unspoken assumption. The Bible reveals a God who adopts various means of communicating to his people, both of a visual and a verbal kind, and to narrow his communication down to one form should be treated with caution. There are several reasons for making such a statement.

First, within the Bible God communicates directly in words and through the messages that his prophets and other messengers speak. But he also communicates through dreams, visions, dramatic actions, carefully composed poetry, song, thinking-aloud-type reflection and, perhaps most commonly, through narratives and history. While today any communication from God must be totally in line with his completed revelation in scripture, why should the means he uses be reduced exclusively to one, even if that one method assumes some measure of priority?

Second, truth compels us to admit that we know remarkably little about the form taken by early Christian preaching to a Christian congregation, on which the contemporary sermon is said to be modelled.[15] The sermons in the Acts are mostly summaries of evangelistic sermons to a Jewish audience, although on two occasions they are addressed to Gentiles, and they leave a good deal unsaid. We can probably reconstruct what Paul's preaching was like from his writings, since these were composed orally and then read to a congregation, but to get from them to what we now call a sermon involves a number of steps and assumptions which we do not often admit. Then again, we can build on what we know about the tradition of synagogue preaching, but our knowledge is limited and our claims should be correspondingly modest. To say the twenty-minute (or whatever length you choose) monologue to believers in a church building which we call preaching is the heir to New Testament preaching may short-change New Testament preaching.

Third, down the centuries God has clearly used other forms of communication as well as the sermon. These include:

- theological disputation and debate, as in the Reformation;

---

15. James W. Thompson, *Preaching Like Paul: Homiletic Wisdom for Today* (Louisville: Westminster John Knox, 2001), pp. 21–27. For a discussion of models of early church preaching, see Hughes Oliphant Old, *The Reading and Preaching of the Scriptures in the Worship of the Christian Church, Vol. 1, The Biblical Period* (Grand Rapids: Eerdmans, 1998).

- Bible translation and the direct, unmediated use of scripture;
- dramatic enactments, such as those pioneered by the prophets;
- writing, such as contemporary evangelistic books, which take their cue from the Gospels;
- even visionary experiences and dreams, for which there is much biblical precedent.

All of these, and more, have played and continue to play a role in the church.

Fourth, forms and style of communication are very much influenced by culture, and many more and different means of communication are available today than previously. None of these are to be used uncritically, some are more effective than others and some are more tainted than others. Modern methods of communication have not taken the Creator by surprise and it would be remarkable indeed if he did not make use of every available medium of communication to broadcast his truth. They all need to be claimed for Christ. As Paul reminded the Corinthians, who were picking and choosing between leaders, 'all are yours, and you are of Christ, and Christ is of God' (1 Cor. 3:22–23). None can claim a monopoly in leadership, nor in the way in which God communicates to his world.

So, to exalt the pulpit and the modern sermon above all other forms of communication and to place them in a supreme place may be to claim too much. Preachers should be careful to apply the image of the church as a body[16] to their own calling. Preachers are more prominent than other members of the church because theirs is the most regular, visible and collective form of communication. But other members of that same body, and other forms of communication, are equally valuable. We should heed Paul's warning that 'our presentable parts need no special treatment' (1 Cor. 12:24): that is to say, they should not be treated differently in terms of honour and status, even though they may require special training. The sermon is a vital tool by which God speaks, but one among others.

The practical impact of how we estimate the value of preaching

Without lessening the responsibility we should feel, or the honour that is ours when called to preach, we frequently need to demonstrate more humility in our estimate of the significance of preaching, especially if we want to know God's blessing on it. How we estimate the status of preaching has a very practical effect on our ministry.

First, *inflated ideas of preaching can lead us to inflated ideas of ourselves.* Whether we intend it or not, as we enhance the status of preaching so we enhance the status of the preacher. Consequently, some preachers see themselves as above the church rather than part of the church. But

---

16. 1 Cor. 12.

preachers are merely members using the particular gifts God has given them among the many others to whom God has given different gifts, all of which are essential to a healthy body. A right estimate of preaching leads us to personal humility, to the deposing of pride and the exalting of grace. It leads us to a more apostolic view of ministry – that 'we have this treasure in jars of clay' (2 Cor. 4:7), or, as Paul puts it in a celebrated put-down, 'What, after all, is Apollos? And what is Paul? Only servants . . . ' (1 Cor. 3:5). Paul's command, 'Do not think you are superior' (Rom. 12:16), applies to preachers as much as to anyone else.

In his much-acclaimed lectures on preaching, Phillips Brooks identified 'self-conceit' as 'beyond all doubt' the first danger that a preacher faces. He explained that,

> in a certain sense every young minister is conceited . . .
> At least every man begins with extravagant expectations
> of what his ministry may result in. We come out from it
> by and by. A man's first wonder when he begins to preach
> is that people do not come to hear him. After a while, if
> he is good for anything, he begins to wonder why they
> do. He finds out that the old Adam is too strong for the
> young Melanchthon.[17]

He continued by explaining that after a time we deal with this initial self-conceit by substituting smaller self-conceits,

17. Phillips Brooks, *Lectures on Preaching*, delivered at Yale Divinity School, 1877 (London: Allenson and Co., n.d.), p. 60.

'some petty pride', as he called it. We become content that
our sermons are commended, or our name is known in our
denomination, or we stress 'the dignity of ordination'. We
say to ourselves, 'I am a minister. I bear a dignity that these
laymen cannot boast. I have an ordination which separates
me into an indefinable, mysterious privilege.' He warned,
'Here is, the beginning of many of the fantastic and exaggerated theories about the ministry. The little preacher
magnifies his office in a most unpauline way.'[18] To avoid
such conceit, Brooks advocated the need for a growing
dedication of one's life to God, and the more and more
complete absorption of our beings 'in seeking God's glory'.[19]

Second, *a correct estimate of preaching reduces the pressure
on the preacher, whereas an overestimate increases the pressure on the preacher*. Again, Phillips Brooks has wisdom to
offer. Having stressed the importance of preparation and
the need to remove, as much as possible, 'the fallible
messenger' from the 'infallible message',[20] he speaks of the
way in which the pressure to preach 'a great sermon' haunts
preachers. This is aggravated when we magnify the importance of 'the sermon'. Such a notion, he says, is fatal. 'It
hampers . . . the freedom of utterance. Many a true and
helpful word which your people need, and which you
ought to say to them, will seem unworthy of the dignity
of your great discourse.' Then he comments, in a way many

18. ibid., p. 63.
19. ibid.
20. ibid., p. 122.

a pastor can recognize from experience, 'Some poor exhorter coming along the next week, and saying it (the true and helpful word that didn't fit into our grand discourse), will sweep the last recollection of your selfish achievement out of the minds of the people.'[21] The simple message from God can cast the grandest pulpit oratory into oblivion. The question we preachers must ask of ourselves is whether we want to be remembered as 'a great preacher', or whether we are content to be a mere messenger for a great God.

Third, *a correct evaluation of preaching magnifies the sovereignty of God.* I have known what is sometimes called 'the romance of the pulpit', that touch of God's Spirit which gives you a fluency beyond your usual powers and wings your words effortlessly into people's lives and transforms them. Yet it is not 'the sermon' that does this, but the Spirit. The same sermon preached on a different occasion may well not have anything like the same effect, as Jonathan Edwards knew. He had preached his revival sermon 'Sinners in the Hands of an Angry God' before and after that special day when it provoked such a reaction in Enfield, Connecticut, on 8 July 1741, but it never had the same impact as it did on that day.[22] It is not 'preaching' as such which is the secret, but the sovereignly free Spirit who chooses on occasion to use preachers.

21. ibid., p. 150.
22. On the sermon, see George Marsden, *Jonathan Edwards: A Life* (New Haven and London: Yale University Press, 2003), pp. 220–225.

Conclusion

We should not glory in preaching. We glory only in the cross of Christ (Gal. 6:14), the message we, as preachers, proclaim.[23] Preaching is not an end in itself and to glory in it as if it were is to make it into an idol. It is neither an automatic panacea for the churches' ills, nor the exclusive means by which people will come to follow Christ. It is one instrument among many, albeit a very important one, which God has given so that we might commend his glory and his glory alone. We cannot do this while simultaneously seeking to glory in ourselves, our calling, or our art. Preachers should never be modest about their message, but should always be modest about themselves and their part in God's work of salvation. Sadly we often mix the two up and display modesty in the wrong place. The gift of preaching, if we have it, is a gift that needs to be offered back to God as a living sacrifice as much as any other aspect of our lives, for that is 'holy and pleasing to God' (Rom. 12:1).

Preacher, keep yourself from idols.

---

23. Older translations of 1 Cor. 1:21 were misleading in implying that 'God was pleased through the foolishness of preaching to save those who believe', as if the method was the point at issue. Recent translations more accurately clarify that what pleased God was the foolishness of the message preached rather than the method used.

2. THE IDOL OF AUTHORITY

During the golden age of the Victorian pulpit it was said that visitors to London would visit the Metropolitan Tabernacle in the morning to hear the Baptist preacher Charles Spurgeon and the City Temple in the evening to hear the Congregationalist preacher Joseph Parker. 'For 35 years,' Alexander Gammie observed, 'Parker reigned in the City Temple like a king on his throne.'[1] Throughout that time he led the City Temple single-handedly, without help from, or accountability to, elders, deacons or a treasurer. He ruled. A close friend of William Gladstone, he attracted massive crowds to both his Sunday services and his Thursday midday service and exercised huge influence, not least over political policy. On one famous occasion which had a direct political impact, in 1899, Parker not only upbraided the Prince of Wales but spoke of the

---

1. Alexander Gammie, *Preachers I Have Heard* (London: Pickering and Inglis, 1945), p. 39.

Turkish-Armenian conflict and thundered, 'He may have been the Kaiser's friend, but in the name of God, in the name of the Father and the Son and the Holy Ghost – speaking of the Sultan not merely as a man, but speaking of him as the Great Assassin – I say, "God damn the Sultan!"'

Those were the days when the pulpit had power and its occupants authority![2] Since then the role of preachers has been marginalized, their status reduced, and it has become commonplace to express reservations about preaching. But this can easily blind us to the real situation. The pulpit is still a very powerful place to stand and people still grant authority to those who stand there, at least within the Christian community. It surprises me how much, rather than how little, preachers continue to exercise great influence over the lives of their listeners.

Contemporary culture has become sensitized to the power dimension in relationships in an unprecedented way and is particularly sensitive to it when people are in a position of trust. Power can so easily be abused, even unwittingly. We have become familiar with the need to check on any potential abuses in dealing with children or vulnerable adults, but we often fail to acknowledge the

2. Although it is interesting that even in the 'golden age of preaching' people were still writing about 'bad preaching', 'dull sermons', 'the declining influence of the pulpit', 'the little success that attends preaching', 'the pulpit in the good old days', and asking, 'Is the modern pulpit a failure?' See Clyde E. Fant, *Preaching for Today* (New York: Harper and Row, 1975), pp. 5–6.

power dimension when it comes to preaching, perhaps in the mistaken belief that it has none.[3]

The rightful authority of the preacher

No genuine preaching is devoid of power and authority.

To speak of authority is not to presuppose a particular style of speech and should not be confused with a 'powerful' manner or declaratory form. Authority is conveyed in many ways – in a gentle and quiet, though confident, manner as much as in a noisy, in-your-face rant. Indeed, sometimes the former is more persuasive than the latter, which can breed suspicion. 'Why is the pastor always angry on Sundays?' was the response of one young member of the congregation to the pastor's 'powerful preaching'.

The authority of the preacher is threefold. First, the preacher's authority resides in the sermon being a declaration of God's word to human beings and therefore God's own authority is inherent within it. His word demands a hearing. The announcement of the gospel calls for a response and cannot just be ignored by listeners. The teaching of apostolic truth equally commands attention

---

3. A rare example of a discussion of the problem of power in relation to ministry generally is found in Paul Beasley-Murray, *Power for God's Sake: Power and Abuse in the Local Church* (Carlisle: Paternoster Press, 1998); and the positive role of the pulpit in church leadership is explored in Michael Quicke, *360-Degree Leadership* (Grand Rapids: Baker Books, 2006).

and calls for a response from believers rather than being met with indifference.

A second source of authority is the anointing of the Holy Spirit, who works in and through the human words of the preacher and in the ears of the listeners to accomplish God's purposes.[4] The work of the Spirit lifts preaching out of the realm of ordinary public speaking or after-dinner entertainment and transforms it into an instrument by which spiritual business is transacted.

Third, the preacher's authority lies in scripture. Preachers are called to 'preach the word' (2 Tim. 4:2) rather than their own thoughts and opinions. When they work to 'correctly handle the word of truth', they are 'approved' by God (2 Tim. 2:15). When they fail to do so, and substitute their own ideas for God's truth, they lose their authority. As stewards of God's grace, we preachers have a real authority, but it does not reside in us personally. It is not ours. It is an indirect authority that comes from our submission to God's word and our faithfulness in transmitting it.[5]

The many biblical images that describe the preacher variously as a prophet, a herald, an ambassador, a teacher and an exhorter all contain overtones of authority. If the preacher is truly the heir of the Old Testament prophet,[6]

---

4. 1 Cor. 3:10–15.
5. See discussion in John Stott, *The Preacher's Portrait: Great Word Pictures from the New Testament* (Leicester: IVP, 1995), pp. 25–26.
6. See P. T. Forsyth, *Positive Preaching and the Modern Mind* (London: Hodder and Stoughton, 1907), p. 3.

as I believe, then the preacher will speak authoritatively in the name of God. Modern preachers do not speak as the Old Testament prophets did about a direct revelation from God, but they speak nonetheless about a sure revelation from God in the Bible with as much conviction as the prophets displayed.

Even if we bow to the culture of our day, with its suspicion of authority, and choose to see preaching primarily in the guise of a 'witness', which is Thomas Long's chosen image for preaching,[7] an element of authority remains. A witness speaks of what he or she saw, heard, learned or experienced, and in doing so speaks with authority.

Strictly speaking, of course, each of these images focuses on the authority of the message, rather than the authority of the messenger, but it is impossible to divorce the two completely. The 'expert' whose words are proved true gains authority, while the 'expert' whose words are discovered to be ill-founded or in some way false loses authority. So it is with preaching.

In the United States, a new (and varied) school of preaching began to gain currency after Fred Craddock published a book called *As One without Authority* in 1974.[8] Increasingly preaching was influenced by what was termed

---

7. Thomas Long, *The Witness of Preaching* (Louisville: John Knox Press, 1989).
8. Fred Craddock, *As One without Authority* (Enid, OK: Phillips University, 1974).

'the New Homiletic'. This advocated that preaching should primarily take an inductive, experiential and narrative form rather than the more traditional form of preaching which was characterized as the transmission of ideas and the desication of the diverse genre of scripture into a set of sterile propositions.[9] But whatever its proponents believe, the new homiletic does not remove the preacher's authority.

The inductive preacher may be said to be 'as one without authority', but it is a myth. The very choice of the question or problem addressed in an inductive sermon, the journey on which the preacher takes the congregation, and the open-ended options with which the congregation may be left makes the preacher an authoritative guide. Preachers who major on experiences raise their own experience, or someone else's, into a place of primacy. Narrative preaching transforms the preacher into a storyteller, but that does not eliminate the question of authority either, whatever may be claimed. The storyteller selects and shapes elements of the story which he or she is telling in order that the listeners may hear or imagine it in a certain way. The storyteller denies the listener access to some parts of the story in order to trace a certain plot or achieve a certain effect. Indeed, part of the appeal of narrative preaching is said to be the influence stories exercise over us.

---

9. A brief introduction can be found in Eugene L. Lowry, *The Sermon: Dancing the Edge of Mystery* (Nashville: Abingdon Press, 1977); and a fuller introduction in Richard L. Eslinger, *The Web of Preaching: New Options in Homiletic Method* (Nashville: Abingdon Press, 2002).

The preacher, then, is in a very powerful position. Every preacher selects, interprets, conveys and applies the message in a particular way. The message may come from God and consequently many people listen to it with care, but it comes through us and not as a direct and unchannelled communication from heaven. When we think of it, it is an amazing sign of the grace of God that he risks trusting his words today, as he has always done, to fallible human messengers.

The abuse of authority

Authority can so easily be abused. The authority of God can too easily become the authority of the preacher; the authority of *the* word can too easily become the authority of *our* words. The power of the gospel can too easily be displaced by the power of human oratory or used to bolster the preacher's status and position. When rightful authority and power become distorted they are on the road to becoming idols.

The abuse of authority in the pulpit takes a number of forms at a popular level, which all those in ministry can readily identify:

- We use the pulpit to preach at people who disagree with us, whether it be over a decision in the church, or over a particular doctrine to which we are committed but about which there are genuine disagreements in the evangelical church.

- We use the pulpit to be dogmatic over issues that belong to the disputed areas, the *adiaphora*, of Christian practice. Romans 14 should caution us to be more limited in our preaching about such issues than we sometimes are. Special days in the Christian calendar, or special experiences of the Spirit, or particular forms of spirituality, mean much to us and so we use the pulpit to impose them on all, even though scripture does no such thing.
- We use the pulpit to go beyond the revelation of God. God has not revealed everything to us, although he has revealed all that we need to know. We forget this and speak authoritatively about the 'secret things', as Deuteronomy 29:29 terms them.
- We use the pulpit to preach as if every issue is of equal importance and never distinguish between what is critical and what is secondary.[10]
- We use the pulpit, increasingly it seems today, to drive our church to adopt our particular vision and plans for growth or development, which often relate to the latest conference we attended, and have more to do with management-speak than biblical truth.
- We use the pulpit constantly to beat up our congregations because we feel they are not supporting us, or our church activities, enough. So we tell them

---

10. I owe this point to Graham Johnston, *Preaching to a Postmodern World: A Guide to Reaching Twenty-First-Century Listeners* (Grand Rapids: Baker Books; Leicester: IVP, 2001).

repeatedly that they could do better in attending, giving, praying, witnessing and so on.

- We use the pulpit to speak well beyond our remit and not only announce the biblical and moral principles of which scripture speaks and which are good for society, but also pronounce on detailed political, social or economic policy.
- We use the pulpit to voice our personal prejudices on everything.

Phillips Brooks warned of the danger in kindly terms when he said, 'We stretch our authority to try to make it cover so much that it grows thin and will not decently cover anything at all. Frankness is what we need, frankness to say "This is God's truth, and this other is what I think."'[11] The truth is that we often not only stretch our authority and make it thin, but move beyond the limits of our authority altogether.

These temptations affect every preacher, but are perhaps particular temptations for itinerant preachers because they are at least one step removed from the realities of congregational life. Consequently, itinerant preachers can make claims, offer promises and utter pronouncements that they know would not hold water if they were having to work day in, day out with a local congregation and were accountable to them. Phillips Brooks advised, 'The sermon must never set a standard which it is not really meant that man

---

11. Phillips Brooks, *Lectures on Preaching*, delivered at Yale Divinity School, 1877 (London: Allenson and Co., n.d.), p. 124.

should try to realize in life.'[12] Too often the preachers who breeze into town and deliver their high-octane addresses do just that, leaving the poor pastor to pick up the debris once they have moved on.

None of this should be taken to mean that our sermons must be limited to spiritual and moral platitudes. God's authoritative word needs to be applied with courage to our contemporary lives both inside the church and out, or else it becomes nice but irrelevant. Care needs to be exercised, however, so that it is the word of God and not our words being applied. Although preaching must touch on every aspect of our lives, we must remember that the commission preachers have is a focused one. Preachers are messengers of Christ to people's 'souls', the deepest and most profound aspect of their humanity. So, although they may be 'ready to speak on any topic of the day', preachers should never give people grounds for mistaking their sermon 'for an article from some daily newspaper'. A sermon, said Brooks, should look 'at the topic from a loftier height, trace trouble to a deeper source and is not satisfied except with a more thorough cure'.[13] Once we stray from this, we abuse our authority and betray our sacred commission. We have no right to either add to or subtract from God's word. Nor should we permit the flattering response of our congregations to cause us to have an overblown view of ourselves and to feed our sense of infallibility so that we assume the

12. ibid., p. 142.
13. ibid., p. 140.

right to speak (or pontificate) on any subject instead of fulfilling our calling.

So then, the pulpit is a place of power and that makes it treacherous, especially if we receive a positive response to our preaching. Congregations can sometimes be guilty of egging preachers on to speak well beyond their remit and preachers can be equally guilty of finding the success of their preaching going to their heads.

At the Keswick Convention in 2000, John Stott, expounding on 1 Corinthians 1:18 – 2:5, ventured that power 'is more intoxicating than alcohol, more addictive than drugs' and that the symptoms of a hunger for power were evident in the church. 'And', he added, 'even in the pulpit, which is an exceedingly dangerous place for any child of Adam to occupy.'[14]

The right exercise of authority

How, then, should we exercise authority?

We should begin by having *a right estimate of ourselves*. We are servants of the gospel who are called to be preachers not because of our natural gifts or impressive personalities, but because of the mercy of God (2 Cor. 4:1). We are no more than 'jars of clay' (2 Cor. 4:7) – perhaps the contemporary image might be disposable plastic cups – who

---

14. John Stott, *Calling Christian Leaders: Biblical Models of Church, Gospel and Ministry* (Leicester: IVP, 2002), p. 41.

contain the message of the gospel. Humility is required if power is not to become an idol.

Second, we must have *a right understanding of our calling.* We are servants of the word and, while we apply that word to a whole range of pastoral situations and contemporary issues, we must be firmly anchored by it. Being anchored to the word will limit our movement, prevent us from straying from our position too much and certainly prevent us from being tossed about by destructive currents. We will learn from Paul to differentiate between saying 'I give this command (not I, but the Lord) . . . ' and 'To the rest I say this (I, not the Lord) . . . ' (1 Cor. 7:10, 12). We will readily accept that while God's word is final, our words are not.

Paul was not afraid to be tentative about a number of issues, including the observance of special days, certain religious practices and meat offered to idols. There was no reason to impose rules about them on fellow believers and every reason to avoid doing so in case it took away their liberty in Christ. He opposed those who sought to impose such rules. Like him, we should seek to apply our Christian minds and pastoral skills to such issues without trespassing on Christian liberty and freedom.

Third, we should have *a right understanding of authority,* which distinguishes between a wise and legitimate authority that derives from our message and a wrong authoritarianism which will immediately be rejected in contemporary culture.

Fourth, we should use *a right measure of power.* The popular understanding of preaching is that what makes it authoritative is that it is 'exciting', 'challenging' or declamatory, and makes an immediate impact.[15] But powerful preaching is to be measured by the long-term effect it has in transforming people's lives and by, to use Jesus' words, producing 'fruit that will last' (John 15:16). In this area two particular forms of preaching that are often considered powerful need to be watched with care.

One form of 'powerful preaching' that needs careful watching is when the preacher rebukes others and denounces error. Congregations who consider themselves to be sound often take delight when the wicked, backsliders and heretics are denounced. One can sometimes almost feel them warming their hands on the fires of hell. On occasions such rebukes may be necessary. Paul censured the false teachers in Galatia with full apostolic authority; John denounced false teachers as 'anti-Christ'; Jude condemned those who threatened the very existence of the church in no uncertain terms. But these attacks related to the very core of the gospel and they are the exception, not the norm.

A second form of so-called 'powerful' preaching which needs to be handled with care is that of exhortation. Of course we will be keen to encourage our congregations to better things, just as the writer of Hebrews does.[16]

15. On the whole question of immediacy, see ch. 9.
16. Heb. 6:9.

Exhortation has its place. But too much exhortation becomes exhausting and, in the end, counterproductive. People need to see *why* they are being encouraged to behave in certain ways, not just be told to do so. People also need to be shown *how* to live life as disciples of Jesus Christ, not just motivated to do so. We forget that Paul spent twelve chapters expounding doctrine in Romans before urging his readers to offer themselves as 'a living sacrifice' (Rom. 12:1). And Hebrews begins with a magnificent and lengthy exposition of the superiority of Christ well before the readers are told not to shrink back and to strengthen their 'feeble arms and weak knees' (Heb. 12:12). Too many preachers look as if they are driving their congregations rather than leading them. Emotional manipulation is not to be mistaken for powerful preaching.

If we take the New Testament as a significant model for our preaching, the staple diet we find there is neither rebuke nor exhortation, both of which are susceptible to the abuse of power, but patient teaching. Time and again, the apostles remind people of what they have come to believe about Christ and then unfold the implications of his gospel both for their personal lives and conduct and for the future of the world. Any authority we have lies in our familiarity with, our understanding of, and our convictions about the gospel. Authority arises from a positive appreciation of the grace of God, not from the negative denunciation of others. If we imitate Paul we will urge as a father (1 Cor. 4:15; 1 Thess. 2:10–11) and only apply the big stick as a matter of last resort. Any discipline we are required to exercise will be administered 'by the meekness and gentleness of Christ' (2 Cor. 10:1).

This is not a matter of tactics, but of theology. God deals with the fault in creation and the sin in our lives not by exercising his power, but by demonstrating his weakness. The cross is at the heart of our message even when, as in Colossians 1, we are confronting the powers and authorities of our world. Our method has to be consistent with our message and calls us to lay down personal status, the lust for power and the craving to be authoritative so that we might represent one to whom all power belongs and yet who was 'crucified in weakness, yet . . . lives by God's power' (2 Cor. 13:4). We are servant preachers of the servant Messiah (Mark 10:45).

Conclusion

Our world is characterized by a lust for power, whether it is the power of the politician, the banker, the lawyer, the bureaucrat or the celebrity. As preachers we are not immune to the same temptations. In fact, since we speak an authoritative message on behalf of a powerful God, and since we play a significant leadership role among his people, we are especially vulnerable to its temptations and can easily be seduced by the very sins we condemn in others. Like any stage, the pulpit contains hidden trap doors through which we might fall. Step by step, the authoritative message becomes the authoritative messenger, and the authoritative messenger becomes the autocratic leader whose word on any issue must be obeyed. It does not take much to distort the rightful authority of the preacher until it is fashioned into an idol. The preacher, no less than others, can become addicted to the recognition, even adulation, which others offer and begin to enjoy the trappings of power. John Stott was right. The pulpit is 'an exceedingly dangerous place for any child of Adam to occupy'.

Preacher, keep yourself from idols.

3. THE IDOL OF POPULARITY

The third idol that lies close to the heart of the preacher is the idol of popularity. It appeals to our yet-to-be-fully-transformed natures. Few of us like to be unpopular and in most of us there remains a deep thirst to be admired. We all like to be liked. Once more, there is a sense in which in some respects this is a perfectly legitimate quest.

Popularity: good and bad

The prophets Isaiah, Jeremiah and Ezekiel were called to preach in the period leading up to and during the exile and they were warned that they would preach to a stubborn people who would reject what they had to say. Indeed, they would be deeply unpopular at times and face personal hardship because of the message they bore. But the New Testament church exudes a different atmosphere. True, Paul struggles with the Corinthians who manifestly do not have as warm a relationship with him as they should have done, but he struggles precisely because their relationship is exceptional. His relationship with the church at Philippi was much closer and warmer, as is evident from his letter, and that is much more typical. The early church is usually portrayed as a place of encouragement and those who lead the church benefited from that encouragement just as much as others did.[1] Leaders were sought out, their addresses listened to eagerly and their letters keenly awaited. Those who benefited from the preachers and teachers were encouraged 'to share all good things with their instructor' (Gal. 6:6), to 'hold them in the highest regard and love' (1 Thess. 5:13), and they were said to be 'worthy of double honour' (1 Tim. 5:17; cf. Phil. 2:29). While all this falls short of saying they were to be popular, it is not far off.

There is a strand of evangelicalism which is so fearful that preachers might get inflated ideas of themselves that it treats them with a measure of disrespect, sometimes almost to the point of rudeness. The 'personality cult' is regularly condemned, and it certainly has to be watched. But the strategies some adopt to keep preachers humble are unworthy. To pray, as happens, 'Lord, thank you for sending Mr A to be our preacher this morning, now blot him out so that we might see Jesus only,' is not as well grounded in biblical truth as the super-spiritual believe.

---

1. Rom. 12:8; Col. 4:8; 1 Thess. 4:18; 5:11, 14; Heb. 3:13; 10:25.

Throughout scripture God uses human messengers, takes full advantage of their splendidly diverse personalities and shows no sign of wanting to eradicate them or their personalities from the story of his people. If Peter and Paul were removed from the book of Acts there would be little left. Unashamedly we are told of crowds that follow them, just as they did their master Jesus. This is in line with the Old Testament, where God even seems to take steps to ensure that people honour his servants Moses and Joshua.[2]

There is a right sense in which preachers should be not only respected, but loved and even popular. Thankfully many are. Why should those who faithfully and competently teach the word of God *not* be loved by those who are Christ's disciples and who hunger to be taught it?

While being loved by and popular with one's congregation may be quite legitimate, even the norm, popularity inherently brings dangers with it, including the risk that it might become an idol. Again, what is good can easily be disfigured, by becoming too prominent in our thinking. When preachers come to love popularity for its own sake it has become idolatrous and a catalogue of errors follow:

- it feeds our egos and takes away from the glory of God;
- it generates pride and removes our dependence on God;

---

2. Josh. 3:7; 4:14.

- it determines our message and we trim the truth;
- it governs our preparation and demotes the importance of scripture;
- it makes us exaggerate for the sake of effect;
- it becomes our security and we stop trusting in God;
- it creates a dependency and reduces our freedom in Christ;
- it becomes our goal and we stop serving God.

To court popularity is to worship an idol instead of the true and living God. Few would do so consciously, at least to begin with, but the idol is subtle and can creep into our lives all unsuspecting until we wake up and realize it has taken over.

The wisdom of John Chrysostom

One of the great preachers of the early church was John Chrysostom. Born sometime between 344 and 354 in Antioch, where he later preached regularly in the cathedral, he became Bishop of Constantinople in 398 and died in 407. As a preacher he was a careful exegete and systematic expositor of scripture. He preached extempore and his style was lively and informal.[3] He was clearly a genius at connecting with his congregation and delighted them with his fierce condemnation of sin and immorality, especially that

---

3. J. N. D. Kelley, *Golden Mouth: The Story of John Chrysostom: Ascetic, Preacher, Bishop* (London: Duckworth, 1995), pp. 57–58.

which was to be found among the powerful, or in the theatre and at the games. He could move deeply the crowds who came to hear him and they frequently broke out in applause.[4] Yet he was not fooled by their response and knew how superficial it could be. Many of his sermons, which were taken down by stenographers, are still in print. Although he could be quite authoritarian, his own verdict on his preaching was modest and revealed a measure of dissatisfaction. 'My work', he wrote, 'is like that of a man who is trying to clean a piece of ground into which a muddy stream is constantly flowing.'[5] His preaching earned him the name *chrysostomos*: that is, 'golden-mouthed'. If anyone knew about popularity and preaching, it was him.

Like us all, Chrysostom was a child of his times and some of his views are ill-suited to modern times. He could be harsh, authoritarian and chauvinist. Nonetheless, in his *Six Books on the Priesthood*,[6] he has tremendous insights

---

4. Philip Schaff, 'Prolegomena: The Life and Work of John Chrysostom', in NPNF, Vol. 9, *St Chrysostom*, ed. Philip Schaff (Grand Rapids: Eerdmans, 1978), pp. 10–11, 22–23.

5. Cited by Donald Attwater, *St John Chrysostom: Pastor and Preacher* (London: Havel Press, 1960), p. 77.

6. The books were supposedly written to his friend Basil to express his dismay at the rumour that they were both to be ordained as priests (or bishops) against their will, as a result of which Chrysostom went missing for a while. Chrysostom explains his inadequacy for the task and in doing so provides a deep and wide-ranging treatise on the work of the priest which includes much wisdom about preaching. It does not read as a work written by an inexperienced youth, but seems to contain his mature reflections on ministry.

into what is required to be a skilled preacher and into the difficulties and temptations preachers face. Many of his insights are as pertinent now as when he lived and not least among them are the observations he offered about the temptations of popularity.

The pulpit, as we observed in the last chapter, is a very powerful platform on which to stand, but its prominence also means that its occupants are subject to a variety of attacks. John Chrysostom wrote of the danger he feared if he was to be ordained as a bishop prematurely. It would be equivalent to being wrecked on a rock inhabited by wild beasts that would savage him relentlessly. What were these beasts? They were the beasts of 'anger, dejection, envy, strife, slanders, accusations, lying, hypocrisy, intrigue, imprecations against those who have done no harm, delight at disgraceful behaviour in fellow priests, sorrow at their successes, love of praise, greed for preferment, teaching meant to please . . . ignoble flattery, contempt for the poor',[7] as well as 'love of praise and desire for honour'[8] – and that was just for starters. It is not, he argued, the job that is to be blamed for these any more than we would argue that 'the sword is to blame for murder, nor wine for

---

7. John Chrysostom, *Six Books on the Priesthood*, trans. Graham Neville (Crestwood: St Vladimir's Seminary Press, 1977), p. 77. An extract from Neville's translation of another section to which I refer in this chapter is found in *The Company of Preachers: Wisdom on Preaching*, ed. Richard Lischer (Grand Rapids: Eerdmans, 2002), pp. 57–63.

8. John Chrysostom, *On the Priesthood*, NPNF, Vol. 9, III.9, p. 49.

drunkenness'.[9] The problem lies within ourselves. We are the ones who should take the blame.

Given the pressures of the ministry, the assaults ministers face, and the awareness of their own frailty and fallibility, it is not surprising that many should seek to comfort themselves by devouring any morsel of encouragement they receive. Such encouragement, as we have seen, can positively nourish us and enable us to develop in our gifts and keep true to our calling. We all know that encouragement is the best soil in which tender plants can grow. But, as Chrysostom recognizes, even good encouragement may become distorted until we develop a dependency on people's praise and make popularity the rule by which we measure all things. We become 'encouragement junkies' with the result that when we receive no positive response or encouraging comments we feel like failures. The absence of verbal encouragement feeds our insecurities and may drive the less robust into depression. When that happens the idol has succeeded in doing its destructive work.

Handling popularity

Chrysostom is particularly insightful in this area. He acknowledges how difficult it is not to be deeply affected by people's response. If they praise, we are elated. If they criticize, we are dejected. He confesses,

---

9. ibid., III.10, p. 49.

This is not easy, my friend, and I think it may be impossible. I do not know whether anyone has ever succeeded in not enjoying praise. If he enjoys it, he naturally wants to receive it, and if he wants to receive it, he cannot help but being pained and distraught at losing it. People who enjoy being wealthy take it hard when they fall into poverty, and those who are used to luxury cannot bear to live frugally. So, too, men who are in love with applause have their spirits starved not only when they are blamed off-hand, but even when they fail to be constantly praised. Especially is this so when they have been brought up on applause, or when they hear others being praised.[10]

If earning praise becomes our ambition, Chrysostom warns, it will be harmful to preacher and people alike. Our preaching will not be for people's improvement, but for their entertainment.[11]

So how should we handle applause and popularity?

First, if we are genuinely seeking to please God and still receive it, *we should not repudiate it*, but receive it with grace and respond to it with discretion.[12]

Second, *we should never seek it*, still less depend on it.[13]

---

10. Chrysostom, *Six Books*, V.4, p. 130.
11. ibid., V.2, p. 128.
12. ibid., V.7, p. 133.
13. ibid.

Third, *we should never be fooled by it* and think that any praise we receive for preaching is a true measure of its worth or effectiveness, because some of the worst preachers receive praise for little achievements while some of the best preachers receive the least praise.[14]

Fourth, therefore, *we need to cultivate a healthy independence from people's opinions*, an independence that must be carefully distinguished from a careless or arrogant indifference. Chrysostom suggested that preachers should be like parents who are neither thrown by their children's 'insults' and 'tears', nor 'think too much of their laughter and approval'.[15] Using another image, he recommends that preachers be like artists who are self-critical of their own designs, but unconcerned about the 'erroneous and inartistic' criticisms of 'the outside world' who do not know what was in their heads when they set out to craft their work. Preachers should also be as indifferent to applause as to criticism. Our aim should be to strive to 'please God' alone, not others.[16]

Fifth, *we should realize that the basis on which people praise us is often faulty.* People 'usually listen to a preacher for pleasure, not profit, like adjudicators of a play or concert'.[17] In doing so they have no wish to be instructed by the preacher and 'they rise above the status of disciples',

14. ibid., V.6, p. 130.
15. ibid., V.4, p. 129.
16. Chrysostom, NPNF, V.7, pp. 72–73.
17. Chrysostom, *Six Books*, V.1, p. 127.

assuming instead the place of mere spectators at a secular rhetoric contest, or even the place of judges.[18] Eloquence and even the reputation of the preacher rather than the content of what is said is often the basis for their judgment.[19] As we would say today, they are sermon tasters! Since this is so, we should not be fooled by their praise.

Sixth, *we should never let it distract us from preaching the truth* and must always strive in our preaching to please God. This alone is our 'rule and determination, in discharging the best kind of workmanship, not acclamation, nor good opinions'.[20] Our task is to defend the faith and announce the gospel, not to entertain audiences.

Seventh, *we should understand that crowds are fickle.* Popularity is a fragile idol and applause soon fades. Chrysostom knew this in his own experience. His forthright preaching led him into trouble more than once. While the masses may have loved him, he made many enemies who conspired against him, and his preaching offended the powerful and led to him being deposed and banished from his episcopal see, not once but twice. He died on his journey home from exile, a journey which has been described as 'a slow martyrdom' for a feeble and sickly old man.[21]

---

18. ibid.
19. Chrysostom, NPNF, V.5, p. 72.
20. ibid., V.5, 6, p. 73.
21. Schaff, 'Prolegomena', p. 15.

To all these, the apostle Paul would surely add that *we need to keep our eye on the one to whom we are accountable* at the end of time. We should preach with care, because 'fire will test the quality of each [preacher's] work' (1 Cor. 3:13). When this ultimate examination occurs, some preaching which proved enormously popular in its day will be shown to have been constructed with cheap materials and will be quickly reduced to a pile of ashes. It will be shown up for what it is, but there will be nothing to show for it of eternal worth.

Conclusion

Popularity is a typical idol: it does not relieve burdens, but becomes a burden; it is a god that is bound to fail and disappoint; it is not worthy of devotion.

When popularity is experienced, when praise comes and applause sounds, they need to be offered back to God.

This first section has reviewed three aspects of the life of the preacher – the pulpit itself, the preacher's authority, and the encouragement preachers might expect. At their best they are gifts of God and positive in their effect, but in the hands of those who are yet to be fully redeemed, they may easily be distorted and made into idols. Since they are close to the very core of our beings and our calling, most preachers are vulnerable to idolize them at some time or another. Good in themselves, when kept in their place, they too easily displace God himself and become rivals to his throne.·

Preacher, keep yourself from idols.

THE IDOLS OF
THE AGE

4. THE IDOL OF SUCCESS

Preaching is always shaped by the context in which it is done. If it were not so it would be a museum piece rather than a living word from God. Although it is often said that what we need today is to preach like Spurgeon or Lloyd-Jones, the truth is that if we did so we would stand out as awkwardly as anyone who chose to wear the clothes of the nineteenth century or the fashions of the 1960s to a day at the office. The sentiment may be right, if it is talking about the gospel they proclaimed, but the substance is wrong. Try reading aloud the sermons of any of the great pulpit giants of the past, and you soon realize how much the style of communication has changed; to say nothing, in Spurgeon's case, of the day of the gas lamp having given way to the age of the electric light and of the empire having given way to globalization and, in Lloyd-Jones's case, to the day of the Second World War and the radio having given way to global terrorism and the Internet and texting.

The gospel is unchanging, but the culture of those to whom it is delivered, and therefore the way in which it is to be delivered, is not.

Even the most ardent traditionalists are not as immune to the influence of their culture as they might believe, and most preachers are at least unconsciously fashioned by their age and their preaching is fashioned by its context. Necessarily so, if it is to communicate. To claim this is not to say that preachers should be captives to their age and slaves to its fashions. Far from it. Any preacher must stand in a position of tension with the age, simultaneously demonstrating engagement with it and distance from it, understanding and yet critical of it.

The apostle Paul serves us well as a model in this regard. On the one hand, he quite genuinely argues, in 1 Corinthians 2:1–4, that he refused to use the eloquence, human wisdom and techniques of persuasion of his day, but 'resolved to know nothing . . . except Jesus Christ and him crucified'. And in 2 Corinthians 4:2 he again distinguished himself from the rhetorical speakers of his day when he claimed to 'have renounced secret and shameful ways' and protested, 'we do not use deception, nor do we distort the word of God. On the contrary, by setting forth the truth plainly we commend ourselves to everyone's conscience in the sight of God.' And yet any analysis of his writing, and of the preaching it reflects, demonstrates that he was a child of his age and, albeit unconsciously, adopted selected rhetorical techniques which would have been common.[1]

So we must engage with, but remain distant from, the culture to which we preach. Failure to keep our distance results in our bowing down to the idols of the age.

What are these idols? I identify four in this section, although there are more: they are the idols of success, entertainment, novelty and secularism.

The idol of success

The more the church has struggled against the forces of secularism, the more the pressure has been heaped on pastors to achieve success. As a result, in some quarters, the church has looked to successful business enterprises to see how that success can be achieved and churches have been turned into business corporations, pastors into CEOs, and spiritual leadership has aped secular leadership.

In the mid-twentieth-century Western world, the church was struggling. It assumed a world that no longer existed and presumed a loyalty which had long since drained away.

---

1. The issue will be explored more fully in ch. 9. Three significant discussions are found in Duane Litfin, *St Paul's Theology of Proclamation: 1 Corinthians 1 – 4 and Greco-Roman Rhetoric*, SNTS Monograph 79 (Cambridge: Cambridge University Press, 1994); James W. Thompson, *Preaching Like Paul: Homiletic Wisdom for Today* (Louisville: Westminster John Knox, 2001); and Ben Witherington III, *New Testament Rhetoric: An Introductory Guide to the Art of Persuasion in the New Testament* (Eugene, OR: Cascade Books, 2009).

The moral consensus had broken down, previously accepted forms of authority were suspect, and more exciting forms of 'fellowship' could be found outside the church than within it.[2] The church had lost its edge and woke up too late to its missionary calling. At the time many pastors claimed that they were merely being faithful and that declining congregations were not their fault but the fault of 'society'. In reality, many were not being faithful at all. They were being nostalgic for a lost world where they enjoyed being a snug fit with members of a self-serving religious club.

Faithfulness and fruitfulness

Being faithful is frequently said to conflict with being successful. Biblically speaking, however, I am convinced that faithfulness will normally result in fruitfulness. There may be exceptional circumstances when faithfulness will lead the church to experience its own equivalent of exile, but this will not be the norm. The New Testament suggests that its normal state will be one of progress and growth. It

---

2. See Callum G. Brown, *The Death of Christian Britain, Understanding Secularisation 1800–2000* (London and New York: Routledge, 2001), and the somewhat different account of Hugh McLeod, *The Religious Crisis of the 1960s* (Oxford: Clarendon, 2007). A more swashbuckling sociological interpretation can be found in Steve Bruce, *Religion in Modern Britain* (Oxford: Oxford University Press, 1995), and a more sober sociological evaluation in Grace Davie, *Religion in Britain since 1945: Believing without Belonging* (Oxford: Blackwell, 1994).

is wrong to oppose faithfulness to fruitfulness: they belong together. In the parable of the vine, for example, Jesus taught that the branches that 'remained' in him would 'bear much fruit' (John 15:8). Immediately following the parable he told his disciples that they had been chosen and appointed to 'go and bear fruit – fruit that will last' (John 15:16). Other parables of the kingdom make the same point in different ways. We have been entrusted with gifts from God which we are to use to enrich his kingdom, not so that we should nervously protect them and return them to him without profit. The servants who gained more through using their initial capital were called faithful. Far from being called faithful, the one who did nothing to augment his master's wealth was condemned as a 'wicked, lazy servant' (Matt. 25:14–30).

Furthermore, as William Willimon has commented in his commentary on Acts,

Making disciples is the job of disciples in Acts. Mainline North American Protestantism, faced with steady decline in membership over most recent decades, tends to waver between superficial techniques for church growth or unconvincing alibis for church death – 'we are not really dying; we are tightening our ranks for service' . . . Luke would not know what to make of a church no longer in the business of making more disciples. While the mission of the church is more than growth, it is not something other than growth. It is certainly not decline. We live in the gracious interim of witness (1:8). In Luke-Acts, any church bold enough to preach the Word, which dares to challenge the cultural status quo, which refuses to accept present political arrangements as eternally given, which is convinced of the truth of its message, which is willing to suffer for the truth will grow. God gives growth to such churches.[3]

In the mid-twentieth-century church, which was not merely static but declining, there was certainly a need for fresh confidence in the gospel, fresh perspectives on mission and uncomfortable questions to be posed about leadership. In that context many turned to the Church Growth Movement,[4] and subsequently to the alluring incentives provided by the seeker-sensitive[5] and mega-church models.[6] The impact of these movements has been significant, if of varying value, as has been their impact on

3. William Willimon, *Acts*, Interpretation Commentaries (Atlanta: John Knox Press, 1988), p. 127.
4. The seminal work which introduced this movement was Donald McGavran, *Understanding Church Growth* (Grand Rapids: Eerdmans, 1970).
5. This became well known through the work of Bill Hybels and the Willow Creek Community Church, South Barrington, Illinois. Among the mass of literature, Bill Hybels, *Courageous Leadership* (Grand Rapids: Zondervan, 2002) is of special relevance.
6. While not directly about the mega-church movement, a key book which relates to the movement and has had an enormous impact is Rick Warren, *The Purpose Driven Church: Growth without Compromising Your Message and Mission* (Grand Rapids: Zondervan, 1995).

preaching. These movements put 'success' unavoidably on the map of ministry.

Critics of the success model

'Success', though perhaps a good thing in itself, is dangerous. Deuteronomy 8:10–20 warned the children of Israel of the dangers of success, fearing that once they settled comfortably in the Promised Land they would forget their Lord and, having done so, would become devoted to other gods and make idols for themselves. A good memory was needed to remind them that their 'success' was purely a gift from God, on whom they were utterly dependent.[7] It was not the result of their own efforts or expertise.

As then, so now. Success, or the desire for it, brings all manner of temptations in its wake. It tempts us to arrogance and to forget the God whose grace has granted us success. It tempts us to pursue the wrong goals for the wrong motives. It tempts us to avoid hardship, weakness, failure, or, in other words, the way of the cross. And when success (or growth) becomes the objective to which everything else must bend, rather than the natural by-product of faithfulness to God, it has truly become an idol. The living God has been displaced.

There is no fiercer critic, or more able theological critic, of the recent trends that have rediscovered success than

---

7. Cf. 1 Cor. 4:7.

David Wells, who in a series of books has wistfully lamented the passing of 'the older role of pastor as a broker of truth'. He grieves over the way in which 'technical and managerial competence' has led to professionalization of the ministry, so that the minister is expected now to be no more than 'a good friend' to his congregation and successful in a manner akin to an entrepreneur or owner of a business.[8] Although David Wells's work suffers from perhaps an over-idealized reading of past culture, his warnings need to be heeded.

The causal connection between the professionalization of the ministry and expectations about preaching, as Wells admits, might be hard to establish, but it seems 'reasonable to assume' such a connection.[9] If success is our goal, it will undoubtedly affect the way we preach. In terms of what we preach it may mean that:

- we are silent on subjects that may prove divisive and unpopular;
- we will be consumed by people's felt needs;
- we will major on the popular topics of the day;
- we will go with the grain of culture rather than be in any way countercultural. We will not want to offend.

---

8. David F. Wells, *No Place for Truth or Whatever Happened to Evangelical Theology?* (Grand Rapids: Eerdmans, 1993), p. 233.
9. ibid., p. 251.

It will also impact the *style* and manner of our communication by:

- replacing expository preaching with topic preaching;
- seeking to cater for the shorter attention span;
- dumbing down the biblical and theological *content* of what we say to cater for a generation of biblical illiterates;
- making entertainment, rather than education, key to our approach.

Wells supports his contention by citing surveys on preaching in contemporary evangelical churches where less than half were shown to be explicitly biblical and 'only 19.5% were grounded in or related in any way to the nature, character, and will of God'.[10]

From a very different angle, Anthony Thiselton, a leading New Testament scholar and theologian, remarked not once but twice, in a recent book on the apostle Paul, on the difference between the style of preaching which is popular today and Paul's preaching.

Whereas much preaching today consists of anecdotes about human life, Paul's preaching was mainly about God, Christ, and the Holy Spirit. Perhaps this is why we easily miss some of the sheer excitement of the gospel.

---

10. ibid., p. 252.

Often today we hear anecdotal sermons about the preacher and his or her experiences. But Paul asserts, 'We do not proclaim ourselves; we proclaim Jesus Christ as Lord, and ourselves as your slaves for Jesus' sake' (4:5).[11]

In a similar way, Ian Stackhouse has pointed out that much contemporary preaching has little understanding of the nature of genuine preaching and because of this 'basic ignorance' consists merely of communicating vision and motivation, both of which are driven by a concern with success. He approvingly quotes Dave Hansen's comment, 'My ideas for the church, even those inspired by the Holy Spirit, have no place in the pulpit; they are not the material of proclamation. Preaching our visions and ideas for the church is cheap leadership, and it is not preaching.'[12]

Hansen has further lamented, 'Preaching clever ideas, church programs, politics and heart-warming stories is thin soup.'[13] Then, in typical fashion, Hansen wisely opined,

While the people of God want desperately to flock to the spiritual food of the word of God, pastors flock to seminars

---

11. Anthony C. Thiselton, *The Living Paul: An Introduction to the Apostle and His Thought* (London: SPCK, 2009), pp. 15, 113.

12. Ian Stackhouse, *The Gospel-Driven Church: Retrieving Classical Ministry for Contemporary Revivalism* (Milton Keynes: Paternoster, 2004), p. 108.

13. David Hansen, *The Art of Pastoring: Ministry without All the Answers* (Downers Grove: IVP, 1994), p. 153.

on how to run church boards, administrate programs and raise up volunteers. They come home with straw to feed their people. Then they wonder why their parishioners are not energized by their new social-scientifically correct leadership methods for manipulating them. Cows don't like being herded into vaccination chutes. People don't either.[14]

My own experience in talking to those in the ministry confirms the picture. Desperate to break out of the failure phase of the church, most have read the latest book on understanding culture, attended the recent most popular conference on how to grow a church successfully, or on how to get young people to come flocking in, or they have adopted the latest programme which seems to guarantee results. Tragically, few have read a Bible commentary or a theology book, although they may have skirted around one just long enough to justify their sermon the following Sunday. They are no longer shaped by scripture, but by technique and the desire for success.

It would seem that the contemporary church too often falls into the trap foreseen by Paul when he wrote, 'the time will come when people will not put up with sound doctrine. Instead, to suit their own desires, they will gather around them a great number of teachers to say what their itching ears want to hear' (2 Tim. 4:3).

---

14. ibid., pp. 153–154.

A way forward

To move beyond the present impasse it is important not to move back to where we were. Justifications of failure and decline, or retrenchment that battens down the hatches against the storms of cultural change in the hope that they will pass, or the resurrection of traditional forms and language for the sake of them, are not the answer. The Bible shows us a God who was always moving forward and addressing the people in the language and culture of the day. As his mouthpieces, so too must we. God did not address his people in exile in the same way in which he did at the high point of the monarchy, or in the Promised Land as he did in the wilderness. Nor did Paul insist on using the form of the synagogue as the place where Gentiles were to be reached with the gospel, and he shifted the language of Jesus as the Messiah in favour of that of Jesus as Lord for the sake of the Gentiles.[15] Our God is not captive to any culture and even less is he a cultural relic.

To move forward, first of all, *we should begin by minding our language.* Language is an extremely powerful instrument which not only helps us express what we believe and experience, but shapes our perceptions at the same time.

---

15. The concept of Jesus as Lord was also meaningful in a different way to Jews, since they referred to God as Lord. See Acts 2:42. Hence my wording 'shifted in favour of', since both concepts were relevant in both cultures, but the balance changed according to the audience addressed.

The vocabulary we choose is significant in helping us understand our experience. There is all the difference in the world between saying 'I applied for this job and got it' and 'God led me to this job and opened the door for me'. The former expresses a secular viewpoint which puts humans at the centre and has no place for God. The latter expresses God's interest and activity in our lives and implies a trust in his providential care as well.

The language of success, although not entirely absent from scripture, comes in our day essentially from the realms of business and politics. It smacks of what we can do to achieve our goals or increase our profits. Biblically, the more relevant vocabulary is the vocabulary of fruitfulness. Fruitfulness comes from the realm of agriculture and keeps our eye focused on the fact that any harvest we experience arises from the life God imparts. We may plant the seed, or water it, and will be duly rewarded for doing so, but it is 'God who makes things grow' (1 Cor. 3:7). The language of fruitfulness, moreover, is organic rather than mechanical or organizational. It is not a programme but life that gives birth to life: that is, the life of God's Spirit working in and through us.

Second, *we should live in the constant tension*, if tension there is, between faithfulness and fruitfulness. We should not seek the former at the expense of the latter. We are called to both. If fruitfulness, as measured by conversions and growing spiritual maturity among our listeners, does not mark our preaching, perhaps we should ask why not?

There may be adjustments we can make to the way we preach that will release fruitfulness without betraying faithfulness. But we should never seek fruitfulness at the expense of faithfulness, as if, in fact, we could. If we are not faithful, we may produce a lot of apparent life, but, like the fig tree Jesus cursed, we may be in danger of producing a lot of leaves but no real fruit.

Third, *we should cultivate a firm grip on the sovereignty of God*, which will have a very positive effect on our preaching. It must never be an excuse for laziness or our lack of fruitfulness. On the contrary, a true grasp of his sovereignty will remind us that he is the sovereign to whom we are accountable and we should therefore use every ounce of gift he has given us to the full. If he is sovereign, our preaching will be marked by diligence both as to its content and in its manner of communication. We will fear lest we do not faithfully pass on the message he has revealed, rather than the message we have created in the image of our own day. And if he is the master who has given us the responsibility of caring for his vineyard, we should do so with an eye to producing a ripe harvest.

At the same time, a firm grasp of God's sovereignty will relieve us of the stress of having to produce results in our own strength. It will also relieve us of the pressure of living up to other people's misguided attempts to judge the effectiveness of our preaching by the measures which this world values, such as popularity, entertainment or mere numerical growth.

Fourth, *we should understand the basis on which God works.* Listening to some leaders today, it almost seems that they have forgotten Christ's promise to build his church and his assurance that 'the gates of death will not overcome it' (Matt. 16:18). I understand their urgency, and agree with it, but they speak as if he has gone back on his promise and that unless they build the church with their strategies, programmes and entertaining preaching, the gates of death will overcome it. We need to recover more faith in him and less faith in our own ideas and plans, while, at the same time, serving him with the utmost diligence.

Conclusion

If 'success' is what drives us, it has become an idol. Ambition, fame, drivenness, a desire for being 'where the action is' and success – all these need to be sacrificed on the altar to God. Time and again, we see in both scripture and history that the people God uses are broken people. It seems, as I myself know, that God frequently has to bring his servants to a crisis point, when they realize that they cannot accomplish anything in their own strength, before their ministry becomes really fruitful. God uses people who are conscious that they do not know the answer rather than those who do, or who know that they are failures rather than those who always seem to succeed. They are the people who look at today's church, as Ezekiel looked at the valley of dry bones, and when God asks them, as he asked Ezekiel, 'Son of man, can these bones live?' They reply, as he did, 'Sovereign LORD, you alone know' (Ezek. 37:3).

Preacher, keep yourself from idols.

5. THE IDOL OF ENTERTAINMENT

I stand in awe of those historians who are able to sum up a whole period of complex history by a short but accurate phrase, such as Asa Briggs's characterization of the late Georgian and early Victorian era as 'The Age of Improvement'.[1] I sometimes wonder how future historians will characterize our own times. Among the variety of suggestions I have is 'The Age of Entertainment'. In celebrity culture, entertainment rules. The leisure, sports and music industries are huge money-making businesses. Films and theatres are mercilessly judged by entertainment value. The ambition of so many young people is to become a pop star or television personality. A teacher wrote recently in a letter to *The Times* that today 'any notion that tedious graft might yield future benefit is rubbished'.[2] Adrenalin

1. Asa Briggs, *The Age of Improvement 1783–1867* (London: Longman, 1959).
2. Ian Slade, 'Letters to the Editor', *The Times*, 7 April 2010.

runs in the veins of city financiers, who are excited about the thrill of making a quick or huge profit (or were, until the financial collapse of 2009 showed how ill-founded the enterprise was). Education has to be fun and even the news is reported with an eye to its entertainment value. If it cannot be said in a soundbite, it cannot be said. The worst sin is the sin of being boring.

Of course, that is to overstate the case. But there is enough truth in it for the picture to be recognizable, and in such a culture many judge preaching by its entertainment value. Preachers do have to take it into account in their preaching, without making entertainment an idol.

The impact of television and the post-television age

Contemporary culture did not arrive with the twenty-first century. It is the product of earlier generations in which the television, which in some respects is now passé, was the most significant shaper of culture. Neil Postman rightly alerted us to the influence of television on culture in his insightfully named book *Amusing Ourselves to Death*, published in 1985.[3]

Earlier, another communications scholar, Marshall McLuhan, had stressed the all-pervasive importance of the media, asserting,

---

3. Neil Postman, *Amusing Ourselves to Death* (New York: Penguin Books, 1985).

All media works us over completely. They are so
pervasive in their personal, political, economic, aesthetic,
psychological, moral, ethical, and social consequences
that they leave no part of us untouched, unaffected,
unaltered. The medium is the massage. Any
understanding of social and cultural change is
impossible without a knowledge of the way media
work as environments.[4]

These two scholars, neither of whom anticipated the
Internet, showed that no medium is a neutral form of
communication, but that whatever medium we choose is
bound to have an impact on the content as well as the style
of what we communicate.

While Postman was chiefly concerned about the television as a visual form of communication, Robert Bellah
highlighted the way in which it has affected our mindset
since it undermines certainty and calls everything into
question. It would be difficult to argue, he said, that television offered any coherent ideology or overall message,
but that is not the whole story. The reality is that 'they do
not support any clear set of beliefs or policies, yet they cast

---

4. Marshall McLuhan, *The Medium Is the Massage* (Harmondsworth:
   Penguin Books, 1967), p. 26. Richard Rorty applied the impact of
   these media directly to the sermon when he wrote, 'The novel, the
   movie, and the TV program have, gradually but steadily, replaced the
   sermon and the treatise as the principal vehicles of moral change and
   progress' (*Contingency, Irony and Solidarity*, Cambridge: Cambridge
   University Press, 1989), p. xvi.

doubt on everything . . . While television does not preach'[5] it is undermining those who do.

McLuhan argued that different media were appropriate for different forms of discourse, but the truth is that one medium, that of broadcasting, has become so dominant that it has affected all other media, including preaching. Television and other forms of recent communication are about bits of undigested information, but even more significantly they are about entertainment and they contribute hugely to this being 'the age of entertainment'.

Television has had the effect of:

- shortening attention spans;
- making everything visual;
- raising standards of professionalism;
- making an art form out of the pretence of moral neutrality;
- spewing out information in an indiscriminate manner;
- reducing everything to being amusing.

The result is that the edge between reality and fantasy has been continuously and dangerously eroded, so that it is often impossible to distinguish between the two. This was epitomized for me when friends caught sight of the planes flying into the Twin Towers on 9/11 as they were entering

5. Robert Bellah et al., *Habits of the Heart: Individualism and Commitment in American Life* (New York, Harper and Row, 1986), p. 279.

the 360° cinema complex at Disneyland, Paris, and assumed it was part of the show. It was not until later that day, when they tried to fly to see us in London, that the reality of the tragedy dawned.

Whatever claims have been made about the impact of television, they have been both exaggerated and compounded by the advent of computers and the Internet.

Responding as preachers

How do we respond as preachers? Several foolish responses need to be avoided. We would be foolish to dismiss the issue as if contemporary culture was irrelevant to us. To respond like the proverbial ostrich and bury our heads in the sand is to condemn preachers to a cultural cul-de-sac. Nor should we merely thunder against our culture and its banality (of which it has plenty) in a purely negative way. We may think we are acting like the Old Testament prophets in doing so, but we must always remember we are called to be messengers of good news. Nor need we be alarmist and agree that preaching has had its day. It has not, or else thousands of people would not still be listening to it, in spite of its variable quality, week after week. There is no social kudos in listening to sermons any more, but people still do, not only as a weekly routine but in droves at special conferences. Nor should preachers uncritically 'go with the flow' and strive to become entertainers themselves. Rather than these blind alleys, our response has to be a considered one. In considering our response, several factors seem to be relevant.

First, *we have a responsibility to speak in a way that communicates in the contemporary cultural context.* To do otherwise is akin to preaching in a foreign language and expecting the Holy Spirit to translate it to the listeners. Given the day of Pentecost in which the Holy Spirit enabled the multi-ethnic audience to hear Peter's words each in their native language (Acts 2:6, 8), this expectation may not be entirely preposterous. God is more than capable of overcoming any lack of cultural awareness in our preaching and in his grace often does so. Even so, to abdicate our responsibility and rely on the Holy Spirit coming to the rescue smacks of laziness. It should never be an excuse for retreating into our hallowed books rather than connecting with our culture. The point to draw from the day of Pentecost is not that God can take our one (cultural) language and translate it to those who speak the language of different cultures, but that God's desire is that all men and women should hear the gospel in language they can understand.[6]

Any knowledge of the history of preaching demonstrates that preaching has adopted various forms over the centuries.

---

6. This is not meant to imply that this is the major 'lesson' to be drawn from the day of Pentecost. It was not recorded as a primer for preachers and much else was happening that day – including the reversal of the curse of Babel through which the nations of the earth, which had been divided by their different languages, were being reunited in Christ.

The allegorical preaching of Origen differed immensely from the Puritan style of preaching in the seventeenth and eighteenth centuries, which differed again from the more recent tradition of black preaching. There has never been one form of preaching, but it has adjusted to the age in which it was delivered and the people to whom it was delivered.

The impact of today's culture on preaching might well take the form of suggesting shorter sermons, a more conversational style, the use of more illustration, whether visual or verbal, and more application. The use of images and visual effects is a complex one and the jury is not yet in a position to give a unanimous verdict as to whether and what sort of visual media will prove effective. To use visual effects badly is almost certainly counterproductive. To use them as a substitute for crafting word pictures and verbal images is a betrayal of the art of preaching.[7]

Second, although it belongs in the general field of communication, *preaching is different from the type of communication that takes place through the media of television screens or computer monitors.* Preaching is a face-to-face act of communication to a live audience (though we may sometimes wonder whether they are alive!). It is therefore a much more interactive form of communication in which the non-verbal signals of the congregation (and

---

7. For this aspect of preaching, see Jolyon Mitchell, *Visually Speaking: Radio and the Renaissance of Preaching* (Edinburgh: T. & T. Clark, 1999).

increasingly verbal interruptions) combine with the response the congregation usually expresses soon afterwards.

Furthermore, preaching is usually done to a community rather than being a private or individual act of communication. This makes it different from the Internet, which is usually an individual activity, and from the television, which at most is usually only watched by a small group like a family. The church community also differs from the audience who gather for a play at the theatre, who are not really a community but usually an unintentional assemblage of people, or at the cinema, where singles, couples or at most small groups watch the big screen in darkness.

The community in which preaching takes place is usually an established community steeped in its own history, traditions, expectations, style, shared beliefs and relationships. As a continuous community where, for the most part, the preacher will be known, relational dimensions of communication, which can never be genuinely matched by the broadcast media, will be evident. In such a relational context our style of communication will take on some aspects of the conversation. Much will be assumed, half-sentences will be spoken and still make sense, the tone will be understood and the impact of personality filtered.

Third, *communication styles are affected by the purpose of communication*. One style does not fit all. Political, technical, financial and academic communication all have their different styles. None of these discourses operate in a vacuum and they are all influenced by the pervasive power of television and the Internet, as any politician hoping to win an election knows, but they are not subsumed by them. Teachers may well have had to make their lessons more entertaining in order to engage an unmotivated bunch of schoolchildren, but they are still dedicated to imparting learning and teaching knowledge and skills that will have a lifelong effect. There is a difference between all these forms of communication and pure entertainment, and the same applies to preaching. As Ecclesiastes might put it, 'There is a time to be entertaining and a time to be thoughtful; a time to be comic and a time to be serious; a time to be amusing and a time to be wise; a time for trivia and a time for the important.'

Fourth, *the average church can never hope to match the quality of presentation mounted by the television.* A large team involving researchers, writers, editors, directors and production people, as well as presenters, puts each programme together. What one sees on the screen is only the tip of a very large iceberg. Preachers usually have to accomplish all this on their own. Being a preacher is very demanding and becomes even more so the moment one wishes to use PowerPoint or any visual input as an aid. Hours can be spent tracking down just the right clip, for no more than a minute in a service, and either hugely lengthens the time taken for preparation, or subtracts time from the serious study of God's word and other aspects of sermon preparation.

Fortunately, churches are not required to match the professional standards of the media, although, again, this is no excuse for amateurism or shoddiness. Two different factors lead me to this conclusion. First, the place of the local church and of preaching within it is much more akin to the numerous community organizations to which people belong than to highly professional national organizations. In comparing preaching in the local church to a television programme we are not really comparing like with like. The true basis for our comparison ought to be the more local, smaller-scale, community-based group. Many such groups still survive and their events continue to attract people in spite of using very poor standards of communication and organization. The local amateur dramatic society still has its attractions in the world of Hollywood. The local football club still has its attractions in the world of the Premiership. And by comparison with many local community groups the organizational and communication skills evident in the church often come over as highly professional!

A second reason for believing that churches need not be intimidated by the professional standards of the media is that there are some signs of a reaction to the highly glossy and professional performances that we associate with it. The Internet, while in some respects continuous with earlier broadcast media, is also significantly different from them. It is an interactive form of communication which involves all the senses. It has democratized 'broadcasting', as the current popularity of YouTube demonstrates. It gives as much freedom for amateurs to broadcast their views as experts and is more comfortable with personal and amateur productions than with highly professional productions that have cost millions of dollars. It makes, of course, no distinction between information that may be reliable and that which is false, but it has freed ordinary people to express themselves in authentic ways, as opposed to the fake and air-brushed images of professionals.

This is already having an impact on the nature of the church and the way it is led and taught.[8] In some circles, the highly professional performances which were associated with some seeker-sensitive events are seen as suspect because they appear to lack authenticity. In an Internet age, authorities are humbled and imagination magnified. Truth is something to be embodied rather than broadcast, to be experienced rather than merely taught. All this gives rise to the importance of local communities and the importance of authentic – but not old-style professional – leaders and teachers. In such a context many a local preacher will be released from the fear of not being able to live up to the media.

Preaching as entertainment

It is time to focus more specifically on the question of preaching as entertainment.

---

8. On the impact of contemporary communication and the reaction to professional presentation of the 'seeker-sensitive' kind, see Robert Webber, *The Younger Evangelicals: Facing the Challenges of the New World* (Grand Rapids: Baker Books, 2002), esp. pp. 61–70.

There can be no justification for being boring when preaching the word of God. There is no virtue in being dull, whatever some preachers may appear to think. One's spirituality is not necessarily increased by tedious sermons, even if it teaches one patience. We have the most exciting of all messages and it is criminal to turn it into an uninspiring, monotonous monologue.

Jesus was evidently the most captivating of speakers. People reported that they were amazed at his teaching and that seems to be as much to do with his style as his content. It was precisely because he did not drone on like 'the teachers of the law' that they sat up and took notice (Mark 1:22, 27; 6:2; 11:18). From the reports of his teaching, we know he had a superb ability to tell stories and an arresting way of teaching even when he was not telling stories. His words were compelling, not least because they arose from a living relationship with God. We cannot be dogmatic about his use of humour, since we are never told in the margins of the script that the crowd laughed, or that this or that saying was a joke. But it is a fair supposition that he used humour and it is hard to imagine that several of his sayings were not treated as comic. His preaching was much more than entertainment for the crowds, but it was nonetheless enthralling.

Modelling ourselves on Jesus suggests to me that we should craft our preaching to be as riveting as our gifts allow, making full use of words that will arrest attention, of stories with which people can identify, and of humour to help lift our serious message and speed it on its way into the hearts and minds of our hearers, just as the airflow lifts a bird and aids it to fly towards its home. Aneurin Bevan, the founder of the British National Health Service, described the maiden speech of Sir Arnold Winrush in the House of Commons as 'the Rolls-Royce of speeches'. It sounded like a compliment until he explained, 'It was smooth, inaudible and seemed to go on for ever.'[9] We should at all costs avoid preaching the Rolls-Royce of sermons.

The idol of entertainment makes no appeal to some preachers. Indeed, they would run a mile from it rather than have anything to do with it, believing their task to be far too solemn. Their fear that their sermons might be contaminated by entertainment may also, in reality, reflect other issues. A significant number of preachers are introverts, more at home with books than people, with ideas than real life. Theological education has often exacerbated such tendencies and turned those who might otherwise be gifted preachers into hesitant and poor communicators.

Other preachers come alive with an audience and feed on the response of the crowd. For them, the idol of entertainment can be a very real temptation. Some preachers seem to have missed their vocation and would bear comparison with the best stand-up comedians of our day. They

9. Mike Fox and Steve Smith, *Rolls-Royce The Complete Works: The Best 599 Rolls-Royce Stories* (London: Faber and Faber, 1984), p. 151.

can use humour as a wonderful weapon with which to pierce the defences of those who are hardened against the gospel. But they should remember that it is a weapon, and all weapons are dangerous. Ammunition can either destroy the enemy or, if not treated carefully, can blow up the one who handles it, or destroy one's allies and comrades in so-called 'friendly' fire. I have heard many humorous preachers entertain an audience to tickling point, but they have done so at the expense of the message they longed to communicate. The laughter went on too long, the right moment to seize the advantage passed, and they lost the battle. Still others were entertaining storytellers. Their sermons were skyscraper sermons: that is, 'one story after another with nothing in between'.[10] They were all communication and no content. 'Such sermons', Haddon Robinson comments, 'hold people's interest but give them no sense of the eternal.' If you find yourself to be naturally entertaining, thank God for a wonderful gift, but keep your eyes wide open to the creeping encroachment of the idol of entertainment.

It is in this area that Phillips Brooks's oft-repeated and wonderfully insightful definition that 'preaching is the bringing of *truth through personality*' needs elaboration.[11]

---

10. Haddon Robinson, 'Blending Bible Content and Life Application', in Scott M. Gibson (ed.), *Making a Difference in Preaching* (Grand Rapids: Baker, 1999), p. 86.
11. Phillips Brooks, *Lectures on Preaching*, delivered at Yale Divinity School, 1877 (London: Allenson and Co., n.d.), p. 5.

He was surely right to insist, 'Let a man be a true preacher, really uttering the truth through his own personality, and it is strange how men will gather to listen to him.'[12] There is even less room for preachers who are not true to themselves today than there was in his day. People soon see through and tire of preachers who affect to be something they are not. Yet we must never shelter behind 'our personality', nor did Brooks intend us to.[13] Our personalities, like every other aspect of our beings, need sanctifying and refining by the Holy Spirit if we are to be preachers fit for purpose and true to our message. Introverts need to learn to love people more and communicate beyond the invisible glass screen that so often seems to separate them from their listeners. Extroverts, natural communicators, imaginative storytellers and comedians need to discipline their natural talents to ensure that they are fit vehicles for the gospel and do not become an end in themselves. Entertaining preachers need to ask whether people go away remembering the stories and jokes, or remembering the Christ to whom they were designed to point. If they only remember the former, we are in danger of having made entertainment our idol.

---

12. ibid., p. 11.

13. Brooks shows that personality is not just to be accepted as it is in saying positively about F. W. Robertson's sermons, 'The personality never muddied the thought. I do not remember one allusion to his own history, one anecdote of his own life; but they are *his* sermons' (ibid., p. 119).

Conclusion

The age in which we live is an age of entertainment and we can learn much from it, though never uncritically, about how to communicate effectively. The Christ whom we serve was the most captivating of preachers and we can learn even more from him about how to accomplish our task. Preaching that entertains may be a culturally appropriate vehicle for the gospel, if the entertainment element is disciplined and kept in its place. However, if we fail to keep it in proportion, if we thrill at the ability we have to entertain, and if that is all we succeed in doing, it has become a deadly weapon and a death-inducing idol.

Preacher, keep yourself from idols.

6. THE IDOL OF NOVELTY

Novelty is a widespread and familiar idol. A society that has brought its children up to be adrenaline junkies, with the expectation that the next emotional experience will outclass the previous one, has inevitably bred a generation of bored, disappointed kids who are always searching for but never finding something new. The 'must have' toys of yesterday are quickly discarded for the 'must have' toys of tomorrow, only for them to be consigned without ceremony to the gadget graveyard and replaced by the latest novelty which will hold our attention . . . well, until the next novelty comes along.

The quest for originality and creativity, which are more respectable words for novelty, is instilled in us by our education system. One of the most damning verdicts that can be passed in any academic context is that we have said or discovered nothing new. The theologian Tom Oden captured the deep effect this has on our subconscious when he wrote, 'I once had a curious dream. The scene was a New Haven cemetery, where I accidentally stumbled over my tombstone, only to be confronted by this bemusing epitaph, "He made no new contribution to theology".' He said he awoke feeling deeply reassured, since he had been trying to follow Irenaeus's command 'not to invent new doctrine'. But his reassurance is another person's insecurity, and he was right to comment on how his attitude ran counter to the educational culture in which he had been formed and what an effort it took to resist the temptation to novelty.[1]

Forms of novelty found in preachers

The worship of novelty may be detected in various ways among preachers. Some reveal it in their early adoption of the latest programme, technique or strategy to be doing the rounds of the conference circuit, as mentioned in chapter 4. Others reveal it in their adoption of new styles of preaching and their attendant untested technology as soon as they are advocated. In this respect novelty often shows itself in the pattern of worship as much as in the sermon. Here, however, we are concerned about two other common guises in which the idol presents itself to preachers. The first is the temptation to new doctrine, and the second is the temptation to new insights on old texts.

---

1. Thomas C. Oden, *After Modernity . . . What? Agenda for Theology* (Grand Rapids: Zondervan, 1992), p. 22.

The first temptation is perhaps less of a temptation for the evangelical who is constitutionally committed to an apostolic gospel and who is temperamentally very suspicious of heresy. Others may be less anchored by scripture and even consciously pursue a new gospel for a new age – a gospel which is often significantly shaped to the latest understanding of the human or physical sciences. For preachers from these wings of the church, where they see a conflict between present-day knowledge and ancient revelation, it is contemporary discovery that wins and ancient wisdom that is sacrificed. This is done without any embarrassment, in spite of the salutary lessons of history. Whatever so-called 'gospel' is developed by this approach quickly becomes outdated as more research is done and the scientific and philosophical communities move on. Dean Inge's famous aphorism applies: 'Whoever marries the spirit of the age will soon find himself a widower in the next.' Who now proclaims the Freudian versions of Christianity, or the death of God, both of which were once vigorously championed as the gospel for the twentieth century?

Evangelicals are not completely immune from such temptations and their commitment to making old doctrines live in contemporary ways makes them vulnerable. Many evangelicals are driven by a passion to make the gospel known and adopt a very pragmatic approach to accomplishing the task. Pragmatism has its strengths, but it may also prove a doubtful friend. Pragmatism has sometimes meant that heresy has been smuggled in under the cloak of mission. Many of the doctrinal deviations of the twentieth century began with a genuine commitment to mission, such as the social gospel movement, some forms of Marxist liberation theology and the gospel's transformation into a form of purely individual, psychological therapy. The history of the Student Movement following the great Edinburgh missionary conference of 1910 should be warning enough.

The less informed and confident evangelical preachers are about the biblical gospel and the more pragmatic they are in their approach to mission, the more vulnerable they are to the wrong sort of novelty. The only way to combat erroneous mission-inspired doctrinal revisionism is for preachers to be doctrinally well informed. Theology needs to be wedded to mission, as it was in the teaching of the Scottish theologian James Denney, who once said, 'I haven't the faintest interest in theology which does not help us to evangelize.' He then explained that this theology would recognize 'the centrality, the gravity, the inevitableness and the glory of the death of Christ'.[2]

Mission equally needs to be wedded to theology, however. Those who are doubtful about the value of theology should consider whether they are happy to allow an electrician who knows nothing about the technical side of the work to rewire their house, or a surgeon who has

2. Cited by R. V. G. Tasker in 'Editor's Preface' to James Denney, *The Death of Christ* (London: Tyndale Press, 1951), p. 8.

not studied medicine to operate on their daughters. Theory has its place. In many spheres it is dangerous to act purely on a pragmatic basis, without any knowledge of theory behind it. So it is with theology, preaching and mission.

The second guise in which the idol of novelty presents itself, however, is more common. It is the desire to find some new angle on the text being preached, to bring out something people have never seen or heard before, and to earn applause for our originality and imagination. Fearing that the text is already too familiar and that the sermon on it may be tired – one that people have heard, or think they have heard, a hundred times before – some preachers examine the text as if they are looking for something that everyone else missed so that they may say something fresh. They approach it with one aim, which is not that they might preach what the text says, but that they might display their expertise in homiletic ingenuity. The novelty often earns plaudits, especially from sermon-tasters. 'I've not seen that in the text before,' they say. When people say that to us it may indicate either that the text has been handled well, or that what was 'seen' was not there to be seen in the first place!

I once heard a good example of this when I listened to a sermon on the letter 'O'. It was based on Daniel 9:4, as in, 'O LORD, the great and awesome God'. To sustain a thirty-minute sermon (it felt longer!) on a single letter requires a great deal of originality and imagination, much of which bears little relationship to the meaning of the text.

It was a poetic masterpiece, but was, truth to tell, spoiled by its total disconnection from the real lives of those who were listening. But what made matters worse was that the word/letter was not in my Bible! It does not appear in some modern translations since it relates to an outdated style. Many sermons that have been rhetorical masterpieces on a single word, or a single verse, which was often very dependent on a particular translation rather than the original, have, in reality, been rhetorical flights of fancy.

C. H. Spurgeon rightly mocked such a preacher when he addressed his students:

> I know a minister whose shoe latchet I am unworthy to unloose, whose preaching is often little better than sacred miniature painting – I might almost say holy trifling. He is great upon the ten toes of the beast, the four faces of the cherubim, the mystical meaning of badgers' skins, and the typical bearings of the stave of the ark, and the windows of Solomon's temple: but the sins of business men, the temptations of the times, and the needs of the age, he scarcely ever touches upon. Such preaching reminds me of a lion engaged in mouse-hunting . . . [3]

Spurgeon warned his students against hovering around the mere periphery of texts and against preaching 'random thoughts' or on 'wayside topics' in place of 'plain

3. C. H. Spurgeon, *Lectures to My Students*, First Series (London: Passmore and Alibaster, 1900), pp. 78–79.

evangelical doctrines'.[4] Our preaching should reflect not only good exegesis, but the importance of a topic given to it in scripture. If we find ourselves preaching a great deal on issues that are not central, because we think that what is central is already familiar, we are in danger of going after novelties.

It should be axiomatic that no sermon should make a secondary issue in the text its main theme. Yet the thirst for novelty often pushes preachers to do just that. To preach, for example, about good parenting on the basis of the parable of the prodigal son is to miss why Jesus told the parable. If we want originality we can do no better, as we shall see below, than study the text carefully. To continue with the prodigal son for a moment, we should be asking why Jesus never told a parable about 'a prodigal son'. His introduction reads, 'There was a man who had *two* sons' (Luke 15:11). How does that impact our preaching? Perhaps we should be preaching on the question, 'Which son was the prodigal?'

Should preachers regularly seek novelty in any of these ways, they are in danger of making it an idol.

The place of novelty in preaching

The warnings against making novelty an idol should not be taken to mean there is no place for novelty in preaching.

---

4. ibid., p. 78.

But, if it is not to assume a life of its own, like the use of imagination it needs to have a conscious and disciplined place in the preacher's approach.

Beginning with the obvious, *preachers need to preach with freshness and deliver their addresses with creative energy*. Preachers whose sermons are a dull monotony, or a tired recitation, or who fail to preach with enthusiasm, or do not speak *as if* what they have to say is a fresh discovery, are not worthy of the calling. Predictability is criminal. Sameness is culpable. That was what the people of Jesus' day accused the teachers of the law of doing. Jesus took the same scriptures as the scribes, but the people reacted to his preaching entirely differently. He spoke with authority – the authority of a real relationship with God – helping the people to see new things in God's word. So too must we. Preaching must involve us in crafting messages that are worth listening to and deserve a hearing. They must apply the true meaning of scripture to the contemporary life of Christians and the ever-changing world in which they live. Otherwise, what is the point? No-one becomes holy by sitting on hard pews and enduring boring, irrelevant messages Sunday by Sunday.

Turning from freshness in delivery, we must ask *what is the place of novelty in content?* Fortunately, Jesus addressed this question specifically in a significant saying in which he was instructing his disciples on how to become teachers in his new kingdom, in contrast to the teachers of Israel who had proved failures.[5] 'He said to them, "Therefore every teacher of the law who has been instructed about the kingdom of heaven is like the owner of a house who brings out of his storeroom new treasures as well as old"' (Matt. 13:52–53).

One implication of this saying is that teachers ought to be able to illuminate their text for their congregations by helping them to understand it more clearly and more deeply than they might do on their own. I recall a very negative reaction by one congregation to a preacher who began his sermon with the words, 'I have been dwelling in this text all week and want to share the fruit of my meditations with you this morning.' He then proceeded to interpret the text in the most shallow and superficial of ways. 'He calls himself a minister,' one member of the congregation protested afterwards. 'His training was wasted on him. I could have got that out of the text after five minutes. What has he been doing all week?' She was right. His devotional thoughts were locked up in the 'old treasures' end of the preaching spectrum and added no 'new treasures' to the congregation's knowledge, or to their faith.

Preachers are teachers and have the responsibility of helping their listeners to appreciate the text more deeply

---

5. A fuller exposition of this and its background can be found in Derek Tidball, *Ministry by the Book: New Testament Patterns for Pastoral Leadership* (Nottingham: Apollos; Downers Grove: IVP, 2008), pp. 25–27.

and to grow in their understanding (Eph. 4:11–15).
'Understanding' certainly encompasses much more than
knowledge of the Bible, as Ephesians makes clear, but it
does not involve less than this, nor does it bypass the
mind.[6] The preacher ought to be able to shed new light on
the text through studying its background, particular
context, location in the wider context of scripture and connection with other scriptures, and in seeking to discover
what it would have meant to those who first heard it. But
then the preacher must avoid the sermon becoming a
historical or theological lecture and must distil this information until there is a clear, relevant and lively word from
God for today. This is a far cry from piecing together a few
blessed thoughts, and an even further cry from the sort of
novel and imaginative preaching which Spurgeon ridiculed
in the quotation above.

This does lead us in the direction of advocating that
expository preaching should be the staple diet of the
church, even if there is a place for variety in preaching
just as there is a place for variety in one's diet. Expository preaching is the most nutritious form of preaching
and the best safeguard against illegitimate novelty. John
Stott has described expository preaching with typical
clarity:

---

6. See the use of the words 'knowledge', 'wisdom', 'discernment' and
   'understanding' which occur frequently in Paul's prayers for the
   church in Phil. 1:9–11; Eph. 1:17–19; 3:14–19; Col. 1:9–10.

To expound scripture is to bring out of a text[7] what is there and expose it to view. The expositor prizes open what appears to be closed, makes plain what is obscure, unravels what is knotted, and unfolds that which is tightly packed. The opposite of exposition is 'imposition', which is to impose on the text what is not there.[8]

Preaching in this way will certainly be considered novel by many congregations who have been fed on a diet of blessed thoughts, imaginative fancies and random ideas which the preacher has brought to the text. It will help them to grasp the message of scripture in entirely fresh ways. There really are plenty of new things that can be legitimately found in the text which have not yet been revealed to the average congregation.

Conservation and innovation

However, the saying of Jesus in Matthew 13:52–53 means more than this. The teachers of Israel whom his disciples were to replace only ever brought old things out of the treasure house of scripture. They parroted the same tired

7. Here and elsewhere, 'text' does not usually refer to a 'verse', which should probably be the exception in preaching, but to the natural unit of the scripture which is more likely to be several verses, a paragraph, a chapter or, especially in the case of some Old Testament narratives, several chapters.

8. John Stott, *I Believe in Preaching* (London: Hodder and Stoughton, 1982), p. 126.

clichés; repeated the same old mantras, stuck fast to inflexible interpretations and wooden understandings. They pored over their documents, but handled them in a lifeless way and never saw the living Christ in them (John 5:38–40). In contrast, the disciples of Jesus were to be true to the scriptures they had received and stand in faithful continuity with them, without contradicting them in the slightest way, yet they were also to bring new treasures out of them.

Matthew himself provides us with the perfect example of how to do this. He takes the life and ministry of Jesus and presents it in a new and highly structured way to answer questions that were thrown up by the conversion of Gentiles who caused some discomfort when they joined the church. He explicitly relates the new to the old by repeatedly referring to the way in which Jesus fulfilled the Old Testament scriptures.

This perspective is not limited to Matthew. It is what all the apostles did as they taught in the synagogues and showed the people how Jesus of Nazareth fulfilled what their scriptures had foretold and that he was none other than the Messiah. We see the same principle at work as they took that same message of Jesus and re-expressed it for Gentile audiences. To obdurate scribes their teaching was a dangerous novelty.

The apostles consistently strove for new ways to express what God had done in Christ. They ransacked both the Old Testament and their own world to press every metaphor they could find into explaining his salvation. It has been suggested that the New Testament contains forty or so such metaphors which are taken from the maternity room (new birth, regeneration), the slave market (redemption), the law courts (justification), the temple (sacrifice and cleansing), the hospital (healing), the family (adoption and reconciliation), the cemetery (resurrection), the school (learning Christ), and so on. Our responsibility remains the same: to express the old gospel in ways that make sense to contemporary men and women.

Furthermore, they constantly had to spell out the implications of the gospel in new ways as they encountered new situations in the early church. The converts in Corinth, for example, posed a whole series of questions that were novel and would never have been raised among Jewish believers: questions about marriage and singleness, eating food sacrificed to idols, how far a believer's ethical liberty stretched, right conduct in worship, and so on. In each case Paul draws them back to the old gospel and applies it in new ways. This too is our task as we confront questions in our contemporary world that have never been faced before.

Here, then, is a model for contemporary preachers. They must first stand in faithful continuity with the message of the Bible and bring out old treasures from the storehouse. There are enough riches already there to be used. There is no need for preachers to *import* new things of their own making into the storehouse, as if its stock were running down, but to stop at bringing out old things is only half the task. Kingdom of God teachers also bring out 'new treasures' – *from* the storeroom. So what are these 'new treasures'? They are fresh expressions of the old gospel and fresh applications of the old message.

David Orton put it well when he said that this is a call 'to be conservative as well as innovative'.[9] Or, as Lancelot Andrewes put it in the seventeenth century, 'we are renovators, not innovators'.[10] We take the old message, but express it in new and fresh ways so that it applies to the contemporary age and culture.

The same balance between continuity and novelty is seen elsewhere. It is implicit, for example, in 2 Timothy 1:13 where Paul instructs Timothy, 'What you heard from me, keep as the pattern of sound teaching, with faith and love in Christ Jesus.' The word 'pattern', according to Donald Guthrie, means 'an outline sketch such as an architect might make before getting down to the detailed plans of a building',[11] which, as John Stott says, implies that 'Timothy must amplify, expound and apply the apostle's teaching', having the pattern, all the time, as the standard by which he measures the truth.[12]

---

9. David Orton, *The Understanding Scribe: Matthew and the Apocalyptic Ideal*, *JSNTS* 25 (Sheffield: Sheffield Academic Press, 1989), p. 152.

10. Cited by John Stott in *Christ the Controversialist* (London: Tyndale Press, 1970), p. 40.

11. Donald Guthrie, quoted in John Stott, *The Message of 2 Timothy: Guard the Gospel*, BST (London: IVP, 1973), p. 45.

12. ibid., pp. 45–46.

Preaching as a reminder

No-one has explored this issue better in recent days than James Thompson has in *Preaching like Paul*. Writing in an American context, he argues that the new homiletic was designed to help preachers speak with freshness to congregations who were already very familiar with the contents of the Bible. It was a way of enabling preachers to avoid predictability, preach creatively and communicate to congregations who had heard it all before. But this is no longer the case, if it ever truly was. Congregations today are no longer as familiar with the message as once they were.

The contemporary challenge is to remind people of the church's teaching, which is in danger of being forgotten altogether, and to educate them by telling them in a more direct way what the Bible says. Preachers often make the mistake of thinking that because they are familiar with the Bible, others must be as well. Preachers often say, 'I can't preach like that because it's too obvious, they'll know all that.' But Thompson understands the situation more accurately when he points out that 'thinking what is shopworn for them is shopworn for others' is an 'occupational hazard' for preachers.[13] It just is not so.

Given this, Daniel Baumann's comment applies even more to today when biblical illiteracy has advanced than when he first made it: 'Anyone who simply sets forth the

---

13. James W. Thompson, *Preaching Like Paul: Homiletic Wisdom for Today* (Louisville: Westminster John Knox, 2001), p. 129.

text and gives its meaning distinctly will be accused of freshness.'[14] We need not fear we will lack novelty if we truly preach the Bible.

This leads Thompson to explore the theme of 'reminding people', which is a primary strategy of communication for the apostle Paul. Typically, in 1 Corinthians 15:1, Paul wrote, 'I want to remind you of the gospel I preached to you,' and this becomes a frequent emphasis in his teaching.[15] He uses this same language even in writing to churches which he had not yet visited, as in Romans 15:15, where he wrote, 'I have written to you quite boldly on some points to remind you of them again . . . ' Other New Testament writers adopted the same approach as Paul.[16] Christians are reminded repeatedly of the tradition they had entered.[17] The teachers of the early church never moved beyond the original apostolic gospel, even though they constantly engaged in making fresh application of it. Time and again they drew people back to the original apostolic gospel and encouraged them to remain loyal to it,[18] while always seeking to make it relevant to the new challenges believers were facing.

---

14. *Leadership*, VI, I (1985), p. 15.
15. See 1 Thess. 1:5; 2:1, 5, 11; 3:3, 4; 4:2; 5:1–2; 2 Tim. 1:6; Titus 3:1.
16. 2 Pet. 1:2; Jude 5.
17. Besides explicit references to 'tradition', such as 1 Cor. 11:23 and 15:3, recalling the tradition is frequent and the use of traditional material is common in Colossians and Ephesians.
18. Gal. 1:8, 9; Phil. 4:9; Col. 2:6; 2 Thess. 2:15; 1 Tim. 4:6; 6:20; 2 Tim. 2:2; 1 Pet. 1:23–25; 1 John 2:7, 24; 3:11; 2 John 5, 6; Jude 3.

Conclusion

So novelty, originality and imagination are important aspects of our task, but there is good and bad novelty, healthy and unhealthy originality, and well-founded and ill-founded imagination. We should never be guilty of perpetrating the bad, the unhealthy and the ill-founded. That is idolatry. We should aim for good, healthy and well-founded forms of novelty. We should never go after novelty for its own sake since that is idolatry, but only when it genuinely serves the communication of the gospel which has been once for all revealed.

We are called to express old truths in new ways, to apply 'timeless' revelation in timely ways and familiar doctrine in fresh colours. The word of God is a living word and not an exhibit of a past age in a museum. We are not called to be parrots, but pastors who take the word of God given once for all and apply it in a lively fashion to people today. The German preacher and theologian Helmut Thielicke put it this way: 'The gospel must be preached afresh and told in new ways to every generation, since every generation has its own unique questions. That is why the gospel must be constantly forwarded to a new address, because the recipient is repeatedly changing his place of residence.'[19]

19. Helmut Thielicke, *How Modern Should Theology Be?* (London: Fontana, 1969), p. 68.

A quotation from P. T. Forsyth aptly summarizes the issue:

> The preacher is not to be original in the sense of being absolutely *new*, but in the sense of being *fresh*, of appropriating for his own personality, or his own age, what is the standing possession of the church, and its perennial trust from Christ. He makes discovery *in* the Gospel, not *of* the Gospel. Some preachers spoil their work by an incessant strain after novelty, and a morbid dread of the commonplace.[20]

Preacher, keep yourself from idols.

---

20. P. T. Forsyth, *Positive Preaching and the Modern Mind* (London: Hodder and Stoughton, 1907), p. 89.

7. THE IDOL OF SECULARIZATION

My choice of the fourth idol of the age may seem surprising, since on the surface preachers would be dedicated to opposing it. It is the idol of secularization. Often unrecognized, this idol is widely worshipped outside the church and has also exercised a pervasive and pernicious influence within the church in recent decades. If preachers do not bow down to it themselves, many in their congregation will and the pressure will mount for preachers, albeit unconsciously, at least to nod in its direction.

Secularization is an extremely tricky concept and handling it is as difficult as keeping hold of a bar of soap when you have wet hands. It has been the reigning paradigm by which sociologists have sought to explain the changing place of religion in the Western world since the 1950s. It is a catch-all concept and that has led to a good deal of confusion in debate. It can refer to the demise of personal religious belief, the decline in religious activity and practice, the marginalization of religious institutions, the disengagement of the church from society, the transformation of religious beliefs into secular concepts, or a disenchantment of the world so that culturally people no longer interpret it in religious terms but in ordinary, everyday, scientific and technological terms. While some still vigorously advocate versions of the paradigm,[1] others have become increasingly uneasy with it and doubt both its validity and its usefulness, given that religion in the West refuses to die, that new forms of spirituality seem to be prolific, and that religion globally has huge political significance.[2]

Our concern here is not to engage with the complex debate, but something much simpler. Whatever the finer points of the argument may be, it is hard to contradict the view that huge changes have taken place in the nations which were traditionally viewed as 'Christian' and these have had a major impact on the way churches function. The old spiritual and moral consensus, however unsatisfactory or superficial it might have been, is no longer in place. Believers live in a different world from their grandparents

---

1. Steve Bruce, *God is Dead: Secularisation in the West* (Oxford: Blackwell, 2002). Bruce has written prolifically on the subject and is heir to his research supervisor Bryan Wilson, who was an early advocate of the theory in his key work *Religion in Secular Society* (London: C. A. Watts, 1966).

2. See, e.g., Peter L. Berger (ed.), *The Desecularization of the World* (Washington: Ethics and Public Policy Centre; Grand Rapids: Eerdmans, 1999).

and this, for good or ill, has in many different ways inevitably affected preaching.

Three aspects of the impact of secularization, loosely defined, will be considered, each of which can encroach on our churches and preaching unless we keep alert.

Pluralism

The first aspect to be considered is that of pluralism. Pluralism is both a social *fact* and a philosophical and political *ideology* and we must be careful to distinguish between the two.

As a social fact, we must accept that the nations of the Western world are multi-ethnic and consequently multicultural and multi-religious. It is foolish to pretend otherwise. The truth is that it has never been any different, but a great acceleration in multi-culturalism has occurred in the last fifty years because of the immigration policies of successive governments. The result is that we live today in democratic societies where the equal political rights of all are respected and none have privileged access to power.

This inevitably has major implications for the place of religion in the public square and nations handle the challenge in different ways. America has resolved it in a very different way from Britain. America's answer has been to welcome the public expression of faiths and find a home for it all under the umbrella of a vague civil religion.

President Eisenhower summed it up well on Flag Day in 1954 when he said, 'Our government makes no sense unless it is founded on a deeply felt religious faith – and I don't care what it is.' Britain's answer has been different. While not as extreme as France, where all religious expression is expelled from the public square, Britain has increasingly marginalized religious discourse and influence in public life, while nominally continuing to doff its cap to the established church and pretending to give all religions a place around the discussion table.

To observe the social fact of pluralism and to grapple with how one deals with it politically, however, is a different issue from having a commitment to the ideology of pluralism with which it is often confused. This ideology is enshrined in our educational system where people are taught to examine everything from everyone's viewpoint, where it is implied that there are no right answers and where anyone who holds a single view-point (unless it is a commitment to the ideology of pluralism, of course) is ridiculed, especially if they hold it strongly. To do so is judged to be narrow-minded and parochial. Our newspapers and broadcasting institutions also propagate the ideology. We have already said that while they claim to preach nothing, they actually cast doubt on everything. From this perspective, pluralism undermines convictions and turns them into mere opinions. It erodes confidence in holding any par-ticular world view or religious belief and these become uncertain and impermanent. Commitments become purely preferences.[3]

As an *ideology and mentality*, rather than a social fact, the commitment to pluralism has come to mean that it is widely thought to be impossible to judge between various beliefs and all are therefore considered to be of equal truth and validity. Connected to this is the way in which our understanding of tolerance has changed. Tolerance used to mean an acceptance of one another and an acceptance of the freedom to disagree with one another. It now means an acceptance of one another and a rejection of the freedom to disagree with one another. The result is that no serious spiritual and moral discussion can be held and all views are granted equal credence and authority, no matter how absurd. The only sin is the sin of dogmatism. In this context the expression of any strong convictions by preachers, however long those convictions may have been held, or however central and even basic to the Christian faith they are, is regarded as unacceptable. Most of all, any claim preachers might make about Jesus Christ as the only Saviour is regarded as arrogant and unacceptable discrimination.

The temptation for preachers in this context is to *react in one of two unhealthy ways*. They may react either by an

---

3. Peter L. Berger, *A Far Glory: The Quest for Faith in an Age of Credulity* (New York: The Free Press, 1992), esp. pp. 39–40, 63–78; Peter L. Berger, Brigitte Berger and Hansfried Kellner, *The Homeless Mind: Modernization and Consciousness* (Harmondsworth: Penguin, 1974), pp. 75–77.

unhealthy accommodation, or by an equally unhealthy resistance, by surrender or defiance. They either capitulate or adopt a defensive bunker mentality. So, on the one hand, preachers may succumb to public pressure and betray the exclusive claims of Jesus Christ,[4] and at the same time begin to jettison other doctrines which are deemed offensive, such as the sovereignty of God, the penal substitutionary interpretation of the cross, and hell. On the other hand, some preachers, probably reacting out of fear, will be pushed into becoming more dogmatic and unreasoning, and start to shout, even scream, their message from a distance, denouncing other people in a way which is not only unattractive but close to inciting religious hatred, even if it does not actually do so. It is wise to avoid both of these extremes.

Preaching in a pluralist world may be a relatively new experience for preachers in the Western world, but it is neither new historically nor unusual globally. In fact, since it is the norm in the church's experience, there are many places where we can look for guidance, including the Acts of the Apostles. Whenever Paul preached in the Gentile world, he confronted pluralism. Christianity, if it existed at all, represented a tiny minority of any city's population and its claims about Christ and pattern of Christian morality would have been subject to widespread derision and often outright persecution as well.

---

4. John 14:6; Acts 4:12.

Take Paul's visit to Ephesus (Acts 19:1–41) as an example. It serves as a helpful model for us. When Paul preached there, the citizens rioted out of fear that his gospel would topple their goddess Artemis and undermine their whole economy. Paul had clearly been uncompromising in his preaching of the gospel, yet the authorities supported him rather than the rioters, saying that he had 'neither robbed temples nor blasphemed our goddess' (Acts 19:37). It was, therefore, the demonstrators, not Paul, who found themselves on the wrong side of the law. As Chris Wright has succinctly said of the incident, 'Clearly Paul's evangelism was uncompromisingly effective but it was not calculatingly offensive.'[5] Similarly, on his earlier visit to Athens (Acts 17:16–33), there is no record of Paul denouncing or ridiculing the beliefs of others. Rather he identifies with them to the extent that he can and then invites people to take a further step on the path they had chosen for themselves as he proclaims the risen Christ.[6] We do not exalt Jesus by putting others down, but by a positive and disarming proclamation of his person and work.

There is no need for compromise in our preaching about the uniqueness of Christ, or in our preaching of other central doctrines of the historic faith. But there is a way of

5. Christopher J. H. Wright, *The Mission of God: Unlocking the Bible's Grand Narrative* (Nottingham: IVP, 2006), p. 181.

6. The sermon on Mars Hill is often somewhat misunderstood. For an excellent explanation of it, see Bruce Winter, 'Introducing the Athenians to God: Paul's Failed Apologetic in Acts 17?', *Themelios* 31.1 (2005), pp. 38–59.

doing it which engages our listeners, and a way of doing it which merely alienates people and puts their backs up. Arrogance and condescension in preaching should not be mistaken for faithfulness. A faithful preacher will model the humility which we see in Christ and the gentleness which his apostles commended.[7] We exalt him both by our winsome preaching and by belonging to communities that embody his truth in their love for each other and for those outside the church.

Relativism

Hand in hand with doctrinal pluralism is ethical relativism and much of what was said under the general heading of pluralism applies to this area as well. Once very much the province of the church, personal ethics are now considered to be, well . . . personal. How one lives is purely a lifestyle choice and a matter of individual preference. 'No-one', we are frequently told, 'has the right to tell me how to live!' Morality has been privatized. If one chooses to live irresponsibly, so be it. Only a few seem to have noticed that the result is that 'society', not the individual, has to bear the cost of the frequent irresponsible and destructive choices made.[8]

---

7. 1 Tim. 6:11; 2 Tim. 2:25; 1 Pet. 3:15.
8. One exception to this is Jonathan Sacks, in *The Politics of Hope* (London: Jonathan Cape, 1997), p. 32, where he brilliantly juxtaposes 'the privatization of morality' with the 'nationalization of responsibility'.

In this context, taking a stand on matters of personal morality is usually considered to be prejudicial or discriminatory. Our culture finds it hard to engage in serious moral conversation and quickly resorts instead to name-calling. Of course, society is never consistent in its handling of such issues, so while the government has continuously de-legislated in areas of family and sexual morality, it has increasingly micro-legislated in terms of smoking, drugs and the place of children and raised other issues, such as the environment, up the agenda.[9]

In this environment, 'preaching' has become a pejorative word. 'Don't preach at me!' is the cry we often hear. The danger is that we react in the same bifurcated way as mentioned above. We either take the fork that leads to surrender and to endorsing whatever the latest moral opinion dictated by public opinion happens to be, or we take the fork that leads to arrogant and insensitive condemnation. The first route leads to *hesitancy*, to uncertain preaching and confused congregations. It is small comfort that Bishop J. C. Ryle wrote at the end of the nineteenth century, 'Old and experienced Christians complain that a vast quantity of modern preaching is so foggy, and hazy, and dim, and indistinct, and hesitating, and timid, and cautious, and fenced with doubt, that the preacher does not seem to know what he believes

9. Sacks again perceptively comments that when a nation stops educating people in virtue they have to fill the vacuum by putting a procedural state in place (ibid., p. 120).

himself.'[10] If it was a problem then, it is even more of a problem now. The second route leads to stubborn defiance of some sort, and this may well lead to professional suicide as far as one's pastoral role is concerned and an inability to guide one's people wisely through the moral chaos in which we live.

Determining our ethical stance may be complex, especially concerning some contemporary question for which there is little historical precedent, and how we do so is beyond the subject of this book. Our concern here is with how our moral stance, once determined, is preached. In that regard, courage needs to go hand in hand with humility, clarity needs to go hand in hand with complexity, or, as John Stott has put it, preachers need to be both authoritative and tentative.[11] We can be authoritative about what God has plainly revealed, but should be tentative where this is not so. Sadly, much authoritative preaching about Christian behaviour merely reflects the practice of the evangelical generation of an earlier age, rather than having foundation in what has been revealed.

I return to the point made in the last chapter that much of Paul's preaching consisted of reminding the early believers of the gospel. There we applied it to the question

---

10. J. C. Ryle, *Principles for Churchmen*, 4th rev. ed. (1900), pp. 165–166, cited by John Stott, 'The Paradoxes of Preaching', in Greg Haslam (ed.), *Preach the Word! The Call and Challenge of Preaching Today* (Ellel, Lancs: Sovereign World, 2006), p. 46.

11. Stott, ibid., p. 45.

of novelty in preaching. Here we apply it to the question of how to preach in a culture where pressure is exerted on us to be diffident and relativistic in our preaching. First, it means we are not obliged to set out a self-contained moral framework that matches the spirit of the age. Rather our task is to relate all our teaching about how to live the Christian life to the gospel. There needs to be an organic connection between ethics and doctrine. Without this we end up as preachers either blown about by whatever winds blow strongest, or merely re-enforcing the empty rules of yesteryear or the kneejerk reactions of today. Without anchoring our teaching in the gospel we leave our listeners feeding on husks instead of the nutritious kernel of truth. We must remember that, to take but one example of a regular pattern, Ephesians 4:1 onwards only makes sense in the light of Ephesians 1 – 3 and its full exposition of the gospel.

Second, as we revisit Paul's strategic use of memory, we need to note the tone he usually adopts. In spite of his apostolic authority, he normally approaches matters sensitively and tries imploring, persuading, urging and correcting with gentleness rather than laying down the law and commanding, as we see, for example, in 2 Corinthians 5. He is prepared to give guidance even where there is no direct revelation, but does so with humility and without abusing his position.[12] Sadly, Christians have often

---

12. 1 Cor. 7:8–16.

been known for being condescending and authoritarian in pronouncing on ethical issues, but such a tone does not commend Christ, especially in a secular culture.

Secularization from within

The third form in which secularization presents itself is the form of secularization from within. One dimension of secularization that has received insufficient attention was identified by Larry Shiner in 1967. It is the way in which religious people transform their spiritual beliefs, behaviour and institutions into purely secular concepts. So, for example, what starts as a firm belief in the imminent second coming of Christ is transmogrified though various stages until it ends up as no more than a belief in human progress. And what begins as a Spirit-filled and focused community of Christ ends up as a mere social club. 'The culmination of this kind of secularization process', he claimed, 'would be a totally anthropologized religion.'[13] His words were, I believe, prophetic. This is the common thread that runs through much of the church, including the evangelical church, since the 1960s. Let me give some examples:

- salvation has become a matter of psychological integration or material comfort;

---

13. Larry Shiner, 'The Concept of Secularization in Empirical Research', *JSSR*, VI (1967), p. 214.

- mission has largely been superseded by aid and development work;
- external divine authority has been supplanted by what feels right to me;
- sin has been translated into sickness;
- moral responsibility has been abdicated by blaming our genes;
- true needs have been dislodged by our felt needs;
- serving our neighbour has been supplanted by individualism;
- faithfulness has been replaced by fitness;
- godliness has been ousted by comfort;
- holiness has been traded in for the feel-good factor;
- the unseen has been overtaken by the seen;
- eschatology has become human progress;
- tomorrow has been shunted out of the way by today;
- eternity has been smothered by the temporal.

A great deal of secularization from within has occurred under the guise of translating the gospel into relevant terms, but in spite of some prophetic voices, like those of David Wells, Os Guinness, Eugene Peterson or William Willimon, it has often been ignored or dismissed as unimportant. Willimon's critique of the way in which so many pastors are seeking to meet the felt needs of their parishioners in their preaching and pastoral care is but one example and is right on target. He writes,

Our culture tends to be a vast supermarket of desire. Anyone who goes out to meet my needs is going to be working full-time!

I believe this is one reason many pastors are fatigued. They are expending their lives, running about in such busyness, attempting to service the needs of essentially self-centred consumers, without critique or limit of those needs.

The gospel is not simply about meeting people's needs. The gospel is a critique of our needs, an attempt to give us needs worth having. The Bible appears to have little interest in so many of the needs and desires that consume present-day North Americans.[14]

The gospel always is and always will be countercultural. Our preaching must enable people to see the world with new eyes, to adopt new mindsets, to deconstruct old world views and reconstruct new ones. This was what we see happening with the disciples, even after three years of Jesus' teaching. On the day of Ascension they were still thinking in old nationalist terms: 'Lord, are you at this time going to restore the kingdom to Israel?' (Acts 1:6). It was what was happening to Peter when he received the vision about clean and unclean food on the rooftop at Joppa (Acts 10:1–23). We are not called to endorse their current world views by adding a thin veneer of spiritual blessing to them.

---

14. William Willimon, *Pastor: The Theology and Practice of the Ordained Ministry* (Nashville: Abingdon, 2002), pp. 95–96.

We are called to bring people to repentance. We are not called to preach so that we might concur with the world, but to convert it; not to chat to it, but to change it; not to ally with it, but to alter it.

In many places an anthropocentric Christianity has been welcomed into the church, but it needs tearing down as surely as Gideon tore down his father's altar to Baal and his father's Asherah pole, and a new altar needs building to the living God, just as surely as Gideon built his altar.[15] It is not in a human-centred gospel but in a Christo-centric gospel that the hope of this world lies.

Conclusion

Secularization is an idol that presents itself in many guises and attracts many worshippers. Even if preachers themselves do not bow down and worship it, they are influenced by the pressure exercised by those in their surroundings who do. We need to keep alert so that we not only avoid the obvious trap of explicitly worshipping it, but also so that we equally avoid being subtly seduced and compromised by it.

Preachers, let us keep ourselves from idols.

---

15. Judg. 6:25–26.

THE IDOLS OF
THE TASK

8. THE IDOL OF ORATORY

We turn in this third section to the potential idols that may be forged by the task or art of preaching itself. Among them are the idols of oratory and immediacy.

Until the advent of Barack Obama I might have thought the idol of oratory was an idol we could safely say had been relegated to the storeroom and was no longer on public display. Sermons used to be crafted as scholarly pieces, often more to be read than heard. Full of erudite learning, literary allusions and rhythmic cadences, they would be vehicles for the display of the oratorical skills of the preacher. The cynic's definition of the sermon as three points and a poem misses the mark as far as these sermons are concerned. They had the poem, but nothing so crude as three points.

The time when preachers could descend from their studies, like Moses from the mountain, and ascend to their pulpit to deliver their artistic creations has long been a thing of the past in many sections of the church, although some fine examples of pulpit oratory remain. These 'fine examples' have often been 'performed' by those whose primary task is that of preaching, as distinct from exercising a more all-round pastoral ministry. For the most part, in line with the homogenization of culture, much preaching in recent days has become informal and conversational, chatty and even sloppy, as if half-prepared, at best, and certainly not in any way crafted by a wordsmith. Even the urging of Eugene Peterson[1] and Walter Brueggeman[2] from their different angles for preachers to become poets has had little effect.

But then came Barack Obama, who captivated his audiences with his oratory and won an election. In doing so he reignited interest in oratory and its significance as an effective means of communication. *The Times* said of Obama's speeches that they 'always seem to take wing. There are two reasons why: the lyrics and the music . . . The flight comes from the rhythm of the sentences, not the elevation of the language.'[3]

An analysis of Obama's acceptance speech in Chicago Fields on the night he won the presidential election in 2008 shows how much he used the classic techniques of

1. Marva Dawn and Eugene Peterson, *The Unnecessary Pastor: Rediscovering the Call* (Grand Rapids: Eerdmans, 2000), pp. 70–73; Eugene Peterson, *Tell It Slant* (Grand Rapids: Eerdmans, 2008).
2. Walter Brueggemann, *Finally Comes the Poet: Daring Speech for Proclamation* (Minneapolis: Fortress, 1989).
3. 'There's music in his words', analysis by Philip Collins, *The Times*, 6 November 2008, p. 20.

oratory.[4] In his case they seemed to ooze out of him naturally rather than to have been drummed into him by media specialists. It was more restrained than much African-American preaching, but exhibited the same features and belonged to the same genre.[5] The key features were as follows.

Key techniques

Contrast

This was heard classically when US president John F. Kennedy famously said, 'Ask not what your country can do for you, ask what you can do for your country.' Obama's acceptance speech included the lines: 'There are mothers and fathers who will lie awake after their children have fallen asleep . . . ' and 'The true strength of our nation comes not from the might of our arms or the scale of our wealth but the enduring power of our ideals.' And he quoted Lincoln, saying, 'We are not enemies but friends . . . '

Three-part lists

Tony Blair spoke of 'Education, education, education.'

---

4. The following analysis owes much to *BBC News Magazine*, 31 July 2009, accessed online.
5. See H. H. Mitchell, *Black Preaching: The Recovery of a Powerful Art* (Nashville: Abingdon, 1990).

Completing the sentence in which he spoke of parents lying awake, Obama said they would do so 'and wonder how they'll make the mortgage, or pay their doctor's bills, or save enough for college'. Or note the sentences, 'So let us summon a new spirit of patriotism, of service and responsibility . . . ' and 'This is our chance. This is our moment. This is our time.'

Imagery

Obama was master of imagery in this speech. He could paint a picture in a few words. He could pull back a curtain on a small window and reveal a whole panorama. For example, he said, 'Our campaign was not hatched in the halls of Washington – it began in the back yards of De Moines and the living rooms of Concord and the front porches of Charleston.' And he addressed himself 'to those who are huddled around radios in the forgotten corners of our world', 'to those who would tear this world down'.

Anecdotes

As one might expect of an American president, many of his anecdotes had to do with the American dream, the belief in the American mythology of log cabin to White House. 'Our stories', he said, 'are singular, but our destiny is shared.' His victory speech told the singular story of the

106-year-old Ann Nixon Cooper and all that she had lived through. It was compelling. With deft brush-strokes he captured people's imagination brilliantly.

Rhythm

Rhythm is a classic hallmark of such rhetoric and is almost certainly more effective than the use of alliteration. 'The road ahead will be long. Our climb will be steep. We may not get there in one year . . . but America . . . we as a people will get there.'

Catchphrase

Many addresses which are hugely effective from an oratorical viewpoint make use of a catchphrase. Obama made use of 'Yes we can'.

The teaching of Jesus

These elements are also found in abundance in the teaching of Jesus, especially in the Sermon on the Mount. His words contained a beauty and rhythm which made ordinary people hear him gladly. His preaching was the very opposite of the mindless meanderings that are sometimes heard in the pulpit today. Take the following very selective illustrations.

Contrast

'You have heard . . . but I tell you . . . ': 'You have heard that it was said, "Love your neighbour and hate your enemy." But I tell you, love your enemies and pray for those who persecute you' (Matt. 5:43–44). 'Lead us not into temptation, but deliver us from the evil one' (Matt. 6:13). 'Which of you, if your son asks for bread, will give him a stone?' (Matt. 7:9)

Three-part lists

In the Lord's Prayer: 'hallowed be your name, your kingdom come, your will be done'; 'Give us today . . . forgive us our debts . . . lead us not into temptation' (Matt. 6:9–13). 'Ask and it will be given to you; seek and you will find; knock and the door will be opened to you' (Matt. 7:7). Elsewhere we read of a lost coin, a lost sheep and a lost son (Luke 15).

Imagery

We read of 'the narrow gate' (Matt. 7:13); the 'wise man who built his house on the rock . . . a foolish man who built his house on sand' (Matt. 7:24–27). Elsewhere Jesus speaks of a camel going 'through the eye of a needle' (Mark 10:25), and of blind guides who 'strain out a gnat but swallow a camel' (Matt. 23:24), and he says, 'We played the pipe for you, and you did not dance; we sang a dirge, and you did not cry' (Luke 7:32).

Anecdotes

One only has to point to the numerous parables to show how important anecdotes were to Jesus.

Rhythm

The rhythm is often somewhat lost in translation, but the Sermon on the Mount has its repeated 'Blessed are the . . . for they shall be . . . ' (Matt. 5:5–10), and equally 'Woe to you . . . ' (Luke 5:24–26). It is also much more evident in the original that the New Testament was written to be spoken in public rather than read silently by an individual. Many rhythms, alliterations and word plays occur, for example, in Ephesians 1 or Hebrews 1.

Catchphrase

'I tell you' (Matt. 5:18, 22, 34; 6:25; 12:6); 'I tell you the truth' (Matt. 8:10; 10:23, 42; 19:28; 21:21), or, as John's Gospel puts it on numerous occasions, 'very truly I tell you' (John 3:3, 5, 11; 5:19, 25; 6:26, 32, 47, 53, and so on). The phrase 'verily, verily, I say unto thee' in the AV and 'truly, truly, I say to you' in the RSV stood out even more.

Historical examples

Older preachers took much more time to craft their words than many contemporary ones who seem busy with so many other things. F. B. Meyer, who was no mean preacher, for example, commented on his own 'habit of mercilessly tearing up page after page [of his manuscript] if I was not satisfied'.[6] Amusingly he added, 'Not infrequently, when I have visited the study of some younger brother in the ministry, I have asked to see his waste-paper basket, being assured that the larger it was the more weighty and successful his ministry would become.'[7]

Looking to the past, we are apt to explain the success of preachers in terms of the blessing of the Holy Spirit and that is an essential element in their effectiveness. Without that, all the oratorical pyrotechnics they could master would never have transformed people's lives. This, however, has sometimes made us overlook the use of oratorical skills by those who have been effective preachers in previous centuries, even though their use seems undeniable. I was somewhat disturbed when I first encountered Harry Stout's biography of George Whitefield, entitled *The Divine Dramatist*. Was Whitefield not a great revivalist who was effective because of the extraordinary power given to him by the Holy Spirit? And was that not a sufficient

6. F. B. Meyer, *Jottings and Hints for Lay Preachers* (London: National Sunday School Union, 1903), p. 74.
7. ibid., p. 75.

explanation of his power? Stout argues somewhat differently. Pointing to Whitefield's experience of the stage, the argument he advances is well summarized in his introduction:

> Given Whitefield's unprecedented success in marketing religion to the eighteenth century, we have to wonder what techniques he employed. My search for an answer took me to a most unexpected and ironic source: the eighteenth-century English stage. [Though church and theatre had been enemies for years] Whitefield managed to fuse a public amalgam of preaching and acting that held audiences spellbound . . . At heart, Whitefield became an actor-preacher, as opposed to a scholar-preacher.[8]

Stout insists that Whitefield introduced a new kind of preaching where the difference between preaching and acting was less distinct than earlier. One of the key differences was due to the understanding of human psychology which came from the theatre but had been lacking in the pulpit. Traditional homiletics assumed the intellect to be supreme and so trained preachers to deliver well-argued, logical and scholarly sermons. In the theatre they believed that feelings reigned supreme. 'It is the passions that harmonize and coordinate intellect and will.

8. Harry S. Stout, *The Divine Dramatist: George Whitefield and the Rise of Modern Evangelicalism* (Grand Rapids: Eerdmans, 1991), p. xviii.

In fact, they control and direct all the faculties.'[9] This is a lesson that still sits ill at ease with theological education and ministerial training where, too often, the emphasis remains on the intellect and the use of rational argument, but not on the management of emotions or the techniques of communication.

The preacher cannot but be a performer and should use, as Whitefield did, every technique of communication that is consistent with the gospel. Some approaches, such as emotional manipulation and subliminal techniques, are incompatible with the gospel of truth. We are obliged to reject the use of underhand methods such as 'deception' or distorting the word of God, but are to set forth 'the truth plainly' (2 Cor. 4:2–3). That, however, is different from recognizing the importance of communication and emotions and working with them, provided that our preaching remains totally consecrated to Christ and reliant on the Holy Spirit.[10]

Paul and the theology of rhetoric

This leads us to a crucial question about the theology of preaching. Does Paul not tell the Corinthians that he shunned the conventional techniques of eloquence of his

---

9. ibid., p. xix.
10. Stout confesses that his approach can easily be taken too far and states that it is 'not meant to supplant or subvert traditional accounts of his piety' (ibid., pp. xxiii, xxiv).

day and 'resolved to know nothing while I was with you
except Jesus Christ and him crucified'? Did he not set aside
'wise and persuasive words' in favour of a 'demonstration
of the Spirit's power' (1 Cor. 2:4–5)? And is the apostle
Paul not our model in this?

Paul's statement needs to be understood in the wider
context of his work and writings.

First, *Paul was a child of his time and reflects, even if
unconsciously, the rhetorical culture in which he lived.*[11]
Whatever explicit claim he makes, his writings and the
record of his speeches provide evidence that he naturally
and frequently used several of the techniques of persuasion
that were taught in the rhetorical schools of his time. The
structure of his letters follows the orderly arrangements
recommended in the oratorical handbooks. He makes
great use of deliberative rhetoric: that is, the sort of rhetoric
used in a political assembly, with a view to persuading
people to take a particular course of action.[12] His writings
exhibit the usual features of arguing from the stand-
point of *ethos* (personal character), *logos* (reason) and
pathos (emotions). He is deductive in his argument,
appealing for transformed behaviour on the basis of
revealed doctrine, and he is middling in style, shunning

---

11. See Ben Witherington III, *New Testament Rhetoric: An Introductory
    Guide to the Art of Persuasion in and of the New Testament* (Eugene:
    Cascade Books, 2009), pp. 10–21.
12. The two other main forms of rhetoric were judicial, as used in the law
    courts, and epideictic, which involved praise and blame.

high-blown rhetoric but occasionally using a plainer, more direct style which is more conversational and lacks careful polish.[13]

What is true of Paul's writings is equally true of the rest of the New Testament, as the work of Ben Witherington III has demonstrated in recent years.[14]

Second, having conceded that, *Paul is clearly not a prisoner of the rhetorical techniques of his day.* Rather than capitulating to the techniques, he stands aloof from them in several respects, and this is the point he makes in 1 Corinthians 2 and elsewhere. Whatever echoes of contemporary oratory may be heard in Paul's writings, he adopts a distinctive approach and does not rely on the usual arts to effect persuasion.

A key difference, as Thompson points out, is that he has a different relationship with his audience than most rhetoricians had with theirs. He writes as an apostle whose message is the result of divine revelation and therefore not subject to the normal criteria of rational proof, which the Greeks would customarily have sought. The unbelieving majority might well, therefore, judge his message to be inferior. As an apostle, he is a 'privileged' interpreter of the gospel and of scripture as it points to a crucified Messiah.[15]

---

13. James W. Thompson, *Preaching Like Paul: Homiletic Wisdom for Today* (Louisville: Westminster John Knox, 2001), pp. 61–84. Fuller argumentation is found in Witherington III, *New Testament Rhetoric.*

14. Witherington III, ibid., *passim.*

15. Thompson, *Preaching Like Paul*, pp. 75–77.

In this respect it is true, as P. T. Forsyth argued in *Positive Preaching and the Modern Mind*, that 'The Christian preacher is not the successor of the Greek orator, but of the Hebrew prophet. The orator comes with but an inspiration, the prophet comes with a revelation.'[16]

A second relevant passage, 2 Corinthians 4:1–6, is probably directed against the false apostles of 2 Corinthians 10 – 13 rather than Greek orators. In it, however, Paul makes essentially the same point as made above, but in doing so explicitly distances himself from their methods of persuasion as well as the content of their message. In a verse to which we have already referred, Paul writes, 'Rather, we have renounced secret and shameful ways; we do not use deception, nor do we distort the word of God. On the contrary, by setting forth the truth plainly we commend ourselves to everyone's *conscience* in the sight of God' (2 Cor. 4:2, italics mine).

Listening to orators was a common sport in the ancient world and was, apparently, increasing in popularity in the first century. Rhetoric was about the art of persuasion and, depending on the school to which they belonged, orators used a number of techniques to achieve their goal, ranging from excessively flattering to brutally berating their

---

16. P. T. Forsyth, *Positive Preaching and the Modern Mind* (London: Hodder and Stoughton, 1907), p. 3. Thompson makes the same point, *Preaching Like Paul*, p. 79. The image needs to be used with some caution as the contemporary preacher is not the recipient of fresh revelation, as were the Old Testament prophets, but the stewards of revelations already given.

audiences. For an orator to commend himself was common, considered acceptable and much appreciated, by his devotees at least. Adapting the message to suit the audience was a fundamental principle of oratory. These are the techniques that Paul says would be inconsistent with the message he was preaching. Style must go hand in hand with substance, and this is the substance: 'For what we preach is not ourselves, but Jesus Christ as Lord' (2 Cor. 4:5). As Charles Cranfield remarked in expounding this passage, 'Of the various temptations which beset the Christian minister, one of the chief and deadliest is the temptation to preach himself.'[17]

Third, after studying the issue in depth, Duane Litfin concluded that it is erroneous to claim the difference between Paul and the Greek orators was that of reason *versus* irrationality, as is sometimes supposed. *The key difference was that Paul refused to use techniques that 'induced' belief in his listeners.* To create faith 'was the sole province of the Spirit of God working through the cross of Christ'. Orators adapted their message so as to 'engineer' a response. The herald's task was not to persuade, but to announce the message. In Paul's case it was to placard the cross so that all could see it.[18] That is our task too.

---

17. Cited in Ralph P. Martin, *2 Corinthians*, WBC (Waco: Word, 1986), p. 81.
18. Duane Litfin, *St Paul's Theology of Proclamation: 1 Corinthians 1 – 4 and Greco-Roman Rhetoric*, SNTS Monograph 79 (Cambridge: Cambridge University Press, 1994), pp. 247–248.

It is false, then, to claim that we need not work at our oratory. For the most part today, we do not work at it enough and we underplay the importance of crafting our words and arguments so as to make them persuasive. Harry Emerson Fosdick was right in saying, 'The preacher's business is not merely to discuss repentance, but to persuade people to repent; not merely to debate the meaning and possibility of Christian faith, but to produce Christian faith in the lives of the listeners; not merely to talk about the available power of God to bring victory over trouble and temptation, but to send people out from worship on Sunday with victory in their possession.'[19] He was right, but one-sided. Oratory does not create the faith in our listeners, the Holy Spirit does.

So we dare not fall into the trap of earlier generations for whom it would appear the display of oratorical skill was the real purpose of preaching. In such times preaching becomes more a means of cultural transmission than a vehicle of spiritual transformation. So let us work, and work harder at the art of persuasion, than we often do. The chief error of the time is probably not that we use too much oratory but too little, not that we overcraft our words but do not craft them enough. At the same time we must always be alert to the way in which oratory becomes an end in itself. We preach because we enjoy the music of the

19. Cited in 'Rhetoric', in William H. Willimon and Richard Lischer (eds.), *Concise Encyclopedia of Preaching* (Louisville: Westminster John Knox Press, 1995), p. 415.

words we produce, rather than because they are instruments of the Spirit's transforming power. When that happens, we find ourselves bowing down to the idol of human words and mere rhetoric.

Preacher, keep yourself from idols.

9. THE IDOL OF IMMEDIACY

Not far distant from the idol of oratory is its nephew, the idol of immediacy. It belongs to a different generation and wears a very different set of clothes, yet curiously it comes from the same family and bears the family likeness since its bloodline is to do with persuasion.

'Immediacy' is the desire for every sermon we preach to be instantly persuasive and have a direct and instant impact. Furthermore, this impact must be demonstrable in measurable ways. There is some impatience with the customary measurements of impact, such as the long-term spiritual growth of the congregation, or even the non-verbal signals which tell a preacher whether the audience is engaged or not, and many today seek for more perceptible expressions by way of a response. Traditional methods of measuring impact are often very vague or elusive. This, in harmony with the managerial spirit of the age, shows that we are producing concrete results. So we measure the effectiveness of our preaching in terms of the response we get to an appeal, or the number who come forward for prayer ministry, the number who seek counsel about the issue we have addressed, or who take some defined action, or even sign up for a programme or prayer letter. The impact we seek is, truth to tell, often psychological in nature as we seek to raise 'feel-good' factor in people's lives. Ironically, this can often be very short term and as vaporous as a deodorant spray.

Appeals: traditional and contemporary

In one sense this desire is not new. It is true that preaching in the revivalist tradition has long been concerned to make appeals for people to 'decide for Christ', often adding 'before it is too late'. Biblical precedent is found in Joshua's challenge to Israel in Joshua 24:15, 'choose for yourselves this day whom you will serve', and in many other places. While in recent history Billy Graham has been the classic exemplar of the approach, he is merely a relatively contemporary example, and a much imitated one, of a longer tradition that may have been re-engineered by Charles Finney but goes back in one form or another to scripture itself.

Such appeals can be well done or cringe-worthy. Of the many examples I have witnessed, perhaps the most comic was that of a preacher who requested 'every head bowed and every eye closed' while he made an appeal for people to signal their desire for conversion by raising their hands. Every head and eye, that is, except those of a colleague who sat on the stage behind him and was required to count the response. The preacher then kept asking his colleague how many had responded and when told the number replied on several occasions, 'Not enough!' He prolonged the appeal until some undisclosed number of respondents which resided in his own head had been reached, at which point we sang the last hymn and were dismissed.

Making such an appeal is not always for conversion and, indeed, these days often is not, but relates to other specific issues such as a commitment to Christian service, a deeper prayer life or financial giving. On one visit to the USA my wife and I heard sermons on the family three weeks running, in three different churches as far apart as Michigan and Florida. Each of these ended with an appeal for husbands and wives to confess failure and recommit them-selves to each other and to signal it by standing or coming forward. When you face such an appeal you are in a dilemma. By responding, are you indicating that you have lacked commitment and need to repair something? By not responding, are you indicating that you do not intend to be committed to your relationship, are in denial about its true state, are arrogantly superior to such calls, or just do not care? On the third occasion, in a 6,000-strong mega-church, I did not stand when called to do so (mainly out of boredom and a feeling of 'here we go again'), nor did my wife (she said, out of loyalty to me). We thought we would be safe as the sermon had been specifically directed to husbands and wives and many in the congregation did not fall into those categories. But the preacher then widened his appeal to include grandparents, children, aunts and uncles, single people who were surrogate aunts and uncles, children and even the family pets (or so it seemed)! The result was that in the end 5,998 people were on their feet, except two inhibited Brits who remained resolutely glued to their seats!

What has changed in recent days is not that we make appeals, but the kind of appeals we make. In many respects our appeals have become less defined, less weighty. Instead of appealing for 'a decision to follow Christ', or conversion, we are often appealing for people to receive 'prayer ministry', or a particular form of the Holy Spirit's blessing or refreshment, or to gain victory in a specific area of our lives. We can measure those who come forward 'for ministry', but often that 'ministry' is of the vaguest kind. It sends its recipients away feeling good, and the preacher feeling even better, but with nothing having fundamentally changed.

The effect of appeals

Setting aside the theological debate about the validity of making appeals,[1] we need to ask what practical effect seeking such an immediate response has on the listener. The effect may well be positive, as it jolts a person out of wrong living to find a new beginning with Christ or a new chapter in their relationship. Many could testify to this. But honesty compels us to admit that more often the effect is short term and may even cause confusion in the respondent. The issues about which we appeal are often not matters that are settled in a moment, but matters that need long-term attention. Responding to an appeal may, and for many does, suggest otherwise.

Over the years I have seen many who were struggling with a moral issue in their lives respond to an appeal, usually at some special event, and assure me the following Sunday, 'It's all right, Pastor, the problem is dealt with. I'm cured.' A week or so later I have found myself picking up the pieces when a moral relapse occurs and a dejected, weak disciple feels that Christ has failed him or her. Equally, I

---

1. There is a legitimate debate in this area with some pointing out, for example, that on the day of Pentecost it was not the preacher but the listeners who made the appeal (Acts 2:37) and that this should be our pattern. Recent publications in the area include Ian Murray, *The Invitation System* (Edinburgh: The Banner of Truth Trust, 1967); R. T. Kendall, *Stand Up and Be Counted* (Grand Rapids: Zondervan, 1984); and Erroll Hulse, *The Great Invitation: Examining the Use of the Invitation System in Evangelism* (Welwyn: Evangelical Press, 1986).

have seen people respond keenly to appeals to become leaders who have no competence in the area and who will never find others following them, or at least not for a considerable time and only after considerable training and formation. But they feel 'called' or even 'appointed' and it is not unknown for some to assert their authority unhelpfully as a result of responding to the appeal. This too can lead to disillusionment. But in these and many other examples, the preacher is able to boast of success and has the kudos of immediate results.

The claim of Christ over our life is urgent and does call for a response. But the quest for an immediate response to our preaching needs to be understood in the context of our instant age. This may reveal that our appeals are not quite as comparable as we might think to the responses that were made in the very different sociological and spiritual context of the New Testament. Our culture is one of individualism, where it is the feeling dimension of the self which drives people. It is marked by transience and impermanence, where we move very quickly from one commitment to another. One only has to look at the way people make their marriage vows to see the point. At one level, bride and groom 'genuinely' promise themselves to each other 'until death us do part'. At another, it is now considered widely unreasonable to expect husbands and wives to live together for life. Marriage that lasts for twenty years and then ends in divorce is increasingly being spoken of as 'successful'. It is a flat-pack society where the furniture of yesterday can be easily replaced by the furniture of today and where the solid, antique furniture of one's grandparents is an embarrassment to all except, in some very select cases, to antiques collectors.

Peter Berger has spoken about our 'homeless minds' which are unable to settle anywhere for long, in respect of beliefs and convictions, and therefore easily get converted and reconverted.[2] Zygmunt Bauman has described the arch symbol of contemporary society as that of 'the tramp' or 'vagrant', always on the move through other people's space. 'The tourist', Bauman says, is exactly the same as the tramp, only wealthier.[3] The result of this is that people respond to appeals in a way that has been shaped by their culture. They respond relatively easily, making what they believe to be a genuine response, but it is not one that necessarily carries any long-term significance.

The biblical response we seek should be one of repentance, a commitment to ongoing discipleship and a life of working through the issues of our previously unregenerate

2. Peter L. Berger, Brigitte Berger and Hansfried Kellner, *The Homeless Mind: Modernization and Consciousness* (Harmondsworth: Penguin Books, 1973).

3. Bauman uses the image in a number of his writings, including *Postmodern Ethics* (Oxford: Blackwell, 1993); *Life in Fragments* (Oxford: Blackwell, 1995); and *Postmodernity and its Discontents* (Cambridge: Polity Press, 1997). For a discussion, see Derek Tidball, 'The Pilgrim and the Tourist: Zygmunt Bauman and Postmodern Identity', in Craig Bartholomew and Fred Hughes (eds.), *Exploration in a Christian Theology of Pilgrimage* (Aldershot: Ashgate, 2004), pp. 184–200.

self. Any lesser response is both superficial and potentially misleading, for it gives the respondent the impression that the matter is dealt with.

Biblical reflections

While the decision to become a follower of Christ may be a decisive event, Paul's letters demonstrate that conversion usually has to be followed by a lengthy process of spiritual and moral re-education whereby the convert learns to live in a Christian way. This involves a long-term and gradual reconstruction of world view as believers stop thinking as infants and as worldly people (1 Cor. 3:1–4; Eph. 4:14–16) and grow up in Christ. It means replacing one's wardrobe, learning to put off one set of behavioural patterns and put on a new set (Eph. 4:17 – 6:9; Col. 3:1 – 4:1). For Paul, it was also essentially a collective issue rather than an individual one, and necessarily so since so much had to do with relationships.

The growth image Paul uses is quite telling. Although growing into adulthood is marked by various stages en route, it does not happen instantly. When the grandparents come to visit they may well say to their pride and joy, 'My! How you've grown. You've shot up.' But for those who live with the growing child daily, growth, for the most part, is gradual and imperceptible. Growth happens not as a result of crisis events, but as a result of good, regular nutrition and healthy exercise. Growth is a by-product of other factors rather than an end in itself. Urging a child to grow is not only useless, but may even be counterproductive if it produces stress. Constantly measuring him or her smacks of impatience rather than wisdom. As with natural growth, so it is with the spiritual growth that occurs through our preaching.

The quest for immediate impact often results from an imbalance between education and exhortation. No-one can deny that exhortation is an important element of biblical preaching. *Parakalein* is used to describe Paul's appealing to Christians to live in a way which is consistent with the gospel. But it always has a basis: 'This imperative can only be properly understood, when it is viewed in the light of the indicative.'[4] We often appeal without having laid the foundation of grace first. I recently heard a sermon, for example, on 2 Peter 1:5–9 by a gifted pastor who was keen to urge his congregation to better things, and rightly so. I had no difficulty with what he said, but I had a grave difficulty with what he did not say. The basis for Peter's exhortation to 'make every effort' was completely ignored. This basis is found in verses 3–4, which tell us about the adequacy of divine power, the certainty of divine promise and the privilege of divine participation that enable us to 'make every effort'. Without that foundation the exhortation is mere despairing moralism. Equally it could be said that verses 10 and 11, which speak of the assurance we

---

4. G. Braumann, 'Exhort', *DNTT*, Vol. 1, p. 571.

have of reaching our destination and of a welcome into 'the eternal kingdom', are relevant. But the enthusiasm to generate better Christian living omitted both sides of the sandwich in favour only of the more immediately exciting 'filling' in the middle.

Our enthusiasm for encouraging Christians to do better can so often be transformed into a burden, unless it is set fully in the context of grace. This means that a regular exposition of the gospel and careful education about the faith need to take precedence over exhortation.

The longing for immediate impact turns our preaching into the equivalent of homiletic fast food. There is a place for it and it proves immediately satisfying to our taste buds. But it quickly leaves us hungry, while creating an appetite for more of the same. In the long term it never satisfies and proves unhealthy. It is immediately more appealing than a square meal of meat and vegetables, but nutritionally deficient over time. Too many congregations are given the fast food of exhortation rather than a more balanced diet of exposition and exhortation.

It is probably largely self-inflicted, but I feel the pressure every week to bow down at the shrine of immediacy and use my gifts and whatever eloquence I have to provoke a measurable response. The pressure is generated by the old sin of pride and it builds up a head of steam as a result of the damaging desire to compare myself to others, rather than being content with the unique ministry I have through Christ. Visible and immediate results would elevate me in the preaching hierarchy and give me celebrity status as one who is exciting and who makes things happen. But it would be deeply damaging to me spiritually and in the long term it would lead to the enfeebling of the church. Rather than encouraging people to grow to maturity in Christ, it would mislead people into thinking there are instant cures which exempt them from costly discipleship and bypass their own responsibility in 'putting off' sin and 'putting on' holiness.

This is exactly the debate Paul had with the Corinthians, who found their 'super-apostles' more attractive than he was. The 'super-apostles' were more entertaining in speech, peddlers of a more attractive message, more successful in their demonstration of acts of power, and they lived a lifestyle more consistent with how worldly people measured success. But Paul denounces them as 'false apostles, deceitful workers, masquerading as apostles of Christ' (2 Cor. 11:13). There was an immediacy and excitement about their way of doing things – but the calculation of effectiveness is not measured today, nor in the short term, but on a day yet to come when the church is presented to Christ (2 Cor. 11:2).

As preachers, the test we face is not that devised by business or management, with its list of tick boxes that measure everything. The test is not that of our congregations, who hanker after visible and immediate results. It is not our own inner and yet to be fully transformed selves, who like to be successful. It is not where we are

placed on a league table of preachers. The test is the eschatological fire to which our work will be subject and which
will reveal the quality of our work as measured in eternal
terms.

The place of seeking a response

My argument is not that there is no place for appeal and
for seeking an immediate and definite response. There is.
My argument is that we should not distort its place and
make it more important than it is. If we seek a response
we should examine our motives carefully and do so with
pure motives, not so that we can feel good about ourselves
and demonstrate our ability to wow others. We should seek
responses that are spiritually significant and not just
psychologically comforting. Above all, we should ask
what the long-term effects will be on those to whom we
make the appeal.

The appeal is necessary, but best made in the context
of a balanced and healthy diet. Donald English said it well:

> There is a kind of preacher whose theological weight is
> such that you are constantly told about a wonderful
> banquet, but never invited to the table or told how to get
> there. There is another kind that constantly and urgently
> invites you to the table and tells you how to come, without
> giving you any sense that what is on the table is worth the
> journey! Our hearers need a theological content that whets

their appetite and a faith content that enables them to enter fully into all that God can be for their lives.[5]

Preaching necessarily involves oratory and appeal, rhetoric and invitation, crafting words and provoking reaction, unchanging truth and urgent response. For preachers to pretend that techniques of persuasion are unimportant is like an engineer who boasts of his ignorance of mechanical physics or a politician who has no interest in winning votes. But the techniques of persuasion are merely tools and should be kept in their place. Any persuasiveness we have is by the grace of God and through the power of the Holy Spirit. Any evidence of it should be judged soundly, according to biblical criteria. Our judgment should neither be influenced by the pretensions of our instant age, nor ever become an end in itself. In other words, it should never become so distorted that it becomes an idol.

Preacher, keep yourselves from idols.

---

5. Donald English, *An Evangelical Theology of Preaching* (Nashville: Abingdon, 1996), pp. 64–65.

THE IDOLS OF
THE MINISTRY

10. THE IDOL OF PROFESSIONALISM

In this final section we discuss some of the wider idols of ministry that have an impact on our preaching. As we do so it is worth remembering that we have a particular perspective on idolatry. We are concerned with that kind of idolatry that takes the form of corrupting what is good by distorting its importance with the result that it becomes a snare. When this happens it demands uncritical loyalty and has become a death-inducing end in itself, rather than a means of serving the living God.

The pressure to be professional

One of the perils of the ministry is that the minister is always considered to be 'the professional'. Whenever the minister is present, he or she is expected to say grace at a meal, or pray at some other function, as if others suddenly lose their tongues. But the expectation of professionalism in ministers is wider than this and can prove daunting. It involves everything from the management of their emotions at funerals, through knowing how to resolve every petty conflict in the church, to knowing how to handle whatever unexpected situation they may encounter.

I was once conducting an open-air service in a beauty spot, with my back to the harbour wall, the sea behind me, facing a crowd of hundreds. Half-way through our programme a woman who had obviously been drinking came and stood beside me and immediately began to undress, with a view to jumping in the harbour. No-one came to my rescue, or to hers, as I was trying to preach the gospel. The stewards watched from the circumference and were either bemused about what to do or enjoying seeing how I would sort the situation out. Perhaps I should have taken Paul's line at Philippi and exorcised her as a trouble-maker immediately! Instead I announced an unscheduled hymn and that gave me some minutes to try to walk her out of the limelight and hand her over to the care of a lady assistant. When I asked my friends afterwards why no-one came to my rescue, they replied, 'Well, they train you for that sort of thing in college, don't they?' I was, in their eyes, 'the professional', so they left it to me. I do not know what they thought we learned in college, but I assure you my training was not so exciting! If every situation like that had been on the curriculum, I would probably still be in training.

The problem is, people always look to preachers to have the right words to say for every possible occasion and we can too easily fall into the trap of enjoying their confidence and rewarding their misplaced faith in us. The result is that we speak when we have nothing to say. We are used to working with words – they are our tools – but we wield them sometimes without purpose or conviction. We are like carpenters sawing wood when they have nothing to make.

The peril of being a professional preacher

By the grace of God, the words we speak when we really have nothing to say may well be used to good effect by the Holy Spirit. Hopefully, too, they are not erroneous words, but display instinctive pastoral wisdom which arises from a life of godliness and a deep knowledge of the scriptures. When we bump into someone carrying a cup, what is inside the cup naturally spills out. So with us, when people bump into us, what is inside us naturally spills out. So even in those unprepared moments when we have to respond spontaneously, we will be in a position to let the Holy Spirit teach us what we should say (Luke 12:12). But this is to put the best interpretation on things.

An indication of the worst interpretation of the perils of being a professional preacher is found in God's condemnation of the false prophets of Israel through Jeremiah. They took advantage of their position and followed 'an evil course and used their power unjustly'. God condemned

them for the way they kept preaching when they had no
authority to do so. His strictures may come uncomfortably
close to reality for many busy pastors. His case against the
false prophets was that:

> They speak visions from their own minds,
> Not from the mouth of the LORD.
> They keep saying to those who despise me,
> 'The LORD says: You will have peace.'
> And to all who follow the stubbornness of their hearts
> they say, 'No harm will come to you.'
> *But which of them has stood in the council of the LORD*
> *to see or to hear his word?*
> *Who has listened and heard his word?*
> *. . . I did not send these prophets,*
> *yet they have run with their message.*
> *I did not speak to them,*
> *yet they have prophesied.*
> *But if they had stood in my council,*
> *they would have proclaimed my words to my people*
> *and would have turned them from their evil ways*
> *and from their evil deeds.*
> (Jer. 23:16b–18, 21–22, italics mine)

A little later God says,

> 'I am against the prophets who steal from one another
> words supposedly from me. Yes,' declares the LORD, 'I am

against the prophets who wag their own tongues and yet declare, "The LORD declares" . . . They . . . lead my people astray with their reckless lies, yet I did not send or appoint them. They do not benefit these people in the least,' declares the LORD. (Jer. 23:30–32)

Preachers have a terrifying responsibility to ensure that they only speak the words the Lord has given. Yet is it, in fact, so terrifying? Does it mean that a preacher should only preach occasionally, after agonizing in prayer and fasting, and studying the word in depth for hours, and only after having a special revelation from God for the congregation? No. The problem with the false prophets was not the time factor. It was the truth factor: they lacked any authentic relationship with God and so could not speak the truth of God. They shaped their message to give people what they knew they would want to hear and they did not bother to check with God whether it was what he wanted them to say or not. Our situation is somewhat different. Although there is the need to seek God for the word which is 'timely', the word that hits the target and matches the need of our hearers, we have the enduring revelation of God in scripture from which to draw. The truth that we are to preach is already revealed, we do not have to make it up. Even so, our relationship with God needs to be maintained if we are to be more than 'mere professionals'.

The key to toppling the idol of professionalism

Preaching, like all ministry, 'is a relationship before it is a task'.[1] Mark's account of the commissioning of the disciples (Mark 3:13–18) is revealing in this respect. The disciples are being sent out 'to preach and to have authority to drive out demons'. Words and works go hand in hand. Persuasive words are supported by convincing acts. But Mark reports a deep paradox in their commissioning. Jesus 'appointed twelve that they might be *with him* and that he might *send them out* . . . ' It shows that ministry is a matter of being and doing, of relationship and of activity. The dual movement of 'being with' and 'being sent out' is at the heart of ministry and care must be taken to maintain the balance. The relationship, once begun, must be guarded with care and never taken for granted. As with any relationship we value, it needs perpetual maintenance. How many have begun ministry spiritually alive and excited by God's word, only to be worn down by its pressures until the relationship with God fades and the perpetual motion of pastoral activity displaces it? Oswald Chambers warned, 'Beware of anything that competes with loyalty to Jesus Christ. The greatest competitor to devotion to Jesus is service for him.'[2] It is

---

1. James R. Edwards, *The Gospel of Mark*, PNTC (Grand Rapids: Eerdmans; Leicester: Apollos, 2002), p. 112.
2. Oswald Chambers, *My Utmost for His Highest* (London: Marshall, Morgan and Scott, 1927), p. 18.

from the position of being in the company of Jesus that
our preaching should flow.

The pressure to be always speaking is a real one and yet
not an impossible one to handle without loss of authenticity. Within recent memory it was standard for a minister
to preach twice on a Sunday and prepare a mid-week address
for the Bible study and prayer meeting. But many would
now say that preaching twice a week, or even once a week
in some cases, is too much for them. Admittedly the admin-
istrative demands of ministry have increased and the pastoral
demands have become more complex, but I was intrigued
to discover that the problem is far from new. Phillips Brooks
addressed it in his lecture in 1877 and responded by saying,

> that a man who lives with God, whose delight is to study
> God's words in the Bible, in the world, in history, in
> human nature, who is thinking about Christ, and man,
> and salvation every day – that he should not be able to
> talk about these things of his heart seriously, lovingly,
> thoughtfully, simply, for two half-hours every week, is
> inconceivable, and I do not believe it.[3]

Of course, if the pressure comes to produce a work of art
every time we speak, to display dazzling oratory or to
mount a virtuoso performance, we shall be in trouble. But
we have already commented on the perils of preaching

3. Phillips Brooks, *Lectures on Preaching*, delivered at Yale Divinity
   School, 1877 (London: Allenson and Co., n.d.), p. 152.

'great sermons' instead of bringing a nourishing word from God to hungry people.[4] Poets only compose a limited number of poems, presidents only make a few memorable speeches, entertainers only have a narrow range of acts, and cooks only serve up a limited number of gourmet meals. Truthfully, the problem I find is not having too little to say, but having too much to say from God's word.

Maintaining a quality relationship with God is what will save us from the lifeless idol of professionalism where words trip off the tongue but have little effect. Closeness to God will release us from the need to live up to other people's unreasonable expectations. It will undermine the desire to present a professional image all the time and will release us to be more authentic preachers.

Closeness to God will free us from the need to know everything and permit us to have space to say 'I don't know' on occasions, although if we say it too often and about issues that people might rightly expect us to know about, such as central doctrines of the faith, our calling to be a teacher in the church might rightly be subject to question. Similarly, closeness to God might release us to admit weakness, vulnerability and failure from time to time. Although, again, this needs to be kept in proportion: if the church's leader is always falling to pieces, why should anyone follow him or her? A third way in which it might release us is in the style of our preaching. Lingering in the presence

4. See pp. 36–37.

of God led the prophets to communicate in a range of different ways, some of them bizarre, and they did not always conform to the way people thought prophets should behave. But it was evident that, however strange their method of communication and however uncomfortable for the religious people who listened, their message came from a genuine relationship with God.

The best sort of professionalism

There are enormous perils in professionalism. However, I believe John Piper overstates the case in his book entitled *Brothers, We Are Not Professionals*, where he claims, 'Professionalism has nothing to do with the essence and heart of the Christian ministry. The more professional we long to be, the more spiritual death we will leave in our wake.'[5] Perhaps. But this can be misleading. In his sovereignty, God is quite capable of using the tongue-tied, like Moses (Exod. 4:10), those who lack professional eloquence, like Paul (1 Cor. 2:1), and those who mangle the English language, as it is claimed D. L. Moody did. But this does not justify shoddiness in our preaching.

---

5. John Piper, *Brothers, We Are Not Professionals* (Nashville: Broadman and Holmann, 2002), p. 1. The issue is, of course, clouded by the way in which we use the word 'professional' in different senses. Technically, 'a professional' is a person who is trained for and engages in an occupation which is based on a body of knowledge, such as theology. To be professional is to reach standards of competence suitable to the profession.

God is no more honoured by our bumbling amateurism than he is honoured by a shallow professionalism. He is worthy of servants who reach high standards, who display competence and produce quality work, not slapdash work, as they serve him. All preachers should develop their skills meticulously to the best of their abilities. For John Chrysostom this meant that those with the greater gifts bore the greater responsibility to exploit them. His words reflect something of the rhetorical context in which he wrote and underestimate the significance of the empowering of the Holy Spirit, nonetheless they make a vital point:

> For though a man has great force as a speaker (which you will rarely find), still he is not excused continual effort. For the art of speaking comes, not by nature, but by instruction, and therefore even if a man reaches the acme of perfection in it, still it may forsake him unless he cultivates its force by constant application and exercise. So the gifted have even harder work than the unskilful. For the penalty for neglect is not the same for both, but varies in proposition to their attainments . . . You see, my dear fellow, that the ablest speaker has all the more need for careful application.[6]

Or, as Jesus put it, 'From everyone who has been given much, much will be demanded; and from the one who

---

6. John Chrysostom, *Six Books on the Priesthood*, trans. Graham Neville (Crestwood: St Vladimir's Seminary Press, 1977), V.4, 5, pp. 130, 131.

has been entrusted with much, much more will be asked' (Luke 12:48).

According to Psalm 78:72, David led Israel 'with skilful hands' and as preachers we might be expected to be skilful speakers who work at our art. The problem comes when that skill is not matched by 'integrity of heart', which is also mentioned in Psalm 78:72, alongside 'skilful hands'. If we seek the wrong kind of professionalism and lack a vital relationship with God, our words become empty. They become merely our own words, dreamed up by our own imaginations and as lifeless as an idol.

Let us aim to be professionals in the best sense of the word, having a mastery of God's word, not in the sense that we are superior to it, but as those who, because we imbibe it deeply, study it regularly and submit to it obediently, can usually apply it appropriately to any situation. But let us shun the idol of sterile professionalism that functions without relationship and makes the mere means of serving God an end in itself.

Preacher, keep yourself from idols.

11. THE IDOL OF BUSYNESS

The compulsive work habits of ministry

Eugene Peterson speaks for many when he describes a difficult patch in his ministry when he wanted to give up. 'Compulsive works habits' had such a grip on him that he was unable to get free of them. His capacity for love and prayer 'had atrophied alarmingly'.[1] In a vibrant American religious economy he had become 'the branch manager of a religious warehouse outlet, who spent his life marketing God to religious consumers'.[2] Underneath it all, he struggled with 'the appalling and systematic trivializing of the pastoral office'. So, like Jonah, he wanted to get off the ship and went to his elders and resigned. He told them,

---

1. Eugene Peterson, *Under the Unpredictable Plant: An Exploration of Vocational Holiness* (Grand Rapids: Eerdmans, 1992), p. 38.
2. ibid.

'I want to study God's word long and carefully so that
when I stand before you and preach and teach I will be
accurate. I want to pray, slowly and lovingly, so that my
relation with God will be inward and honest. And I want
to be with you, often and leisurely, so that we can
recognize each other as close companions on the way of the
cross and be available for counsel and encouragement of
each other. These were what I had started out intending
when I became a pastor, but working in and for the church
has pushed them to the fringes.'

One elder said, with some astonishment, 'If that is what
you want to do, why don't you do it' . . . And I, with a
touch of anger, said, 'Because I have to run the church.
Do you realize that running the church is a full-time job?
There is simply no time to be a pastor.'

Another elder said, 'Why don't you let us run the
church?' I said, 'You don't know how.' He said, 'It sounds
to me like you don't know how to be a pastor either. How
about you let us learn to run the church and we let you
learn how to be a pastor?'

It was one of those wonderful moments in the life
of the church when the heavens open and the dove
descends.[3]

Peterson holds 'the idolatry of a religious career' as respon-
sible for his malaise. Pastors cannot pastor, he protests,

---

3. ibid., p. 39.

because 'we are awash in (that) idolatry' instead of
being immersed in its opposite, namely 'vocational
holiness'.[4]

Although a generalization, it would seem that most
ministers have become the managers of religious organizations rather than exercising the pastoral vocation to
which they felt called. Many would argue that the
change is unavoidable since the task is so open-ended,
the expectations of people have risen, the demands of
legislation and bureaucracy have increased, at the same
time as the availability of volunteers has declined because
of mobility and because the demands on people's lives
outside the church have increased. But ministers can be
their own worst enemies.[5] We want to be needed. We
feel compelled to be instantly available. We feel failures
if we take time out from active engagement. We have
to have a finger in every pie in the church. We find it
difficult to delegate. We like to be in charge. We can
sometimes work inefficiently: failing to work smarter, we
work longer.

All this begins to accumulate and before long we lose
sight of our calling and surrender to the instant and the
immediate rather than having any long-term vision, let
alone eschatological vision, which informs and determines
our priorities. Genuine and healthy hard work has

---

4. ibid., p. 4.
5. The opposite, of course, can also be true. The ministry provides some
   ministers with an opportunity to indulge in laziness.

transmogrified into workaholism and become an idol we slavishly worship.

The effect on preaching

In such a situation, preaching is often relegated to the 'Any Other Business' item on our agenda, the thing we do when we have done everything else, if we have time (which we often have not). For many, preaching at best becomes a question of scraping a sermon together late in the week so we have something to say on Sunday. We become practised at the art of cobbling together a few blessed thoughts to fool the faithful and keep them happy. I have heard many a sermon, and preached a few, which suffered from being given insufficient preparation time. Sometimes this is evident because it simply has not been thought through. Sometimes, sadly, it is evident because the sermon is just padding and waffle, without substance. In some cases, where the preacher is theologically articulate, it is evident because, while the ingredients have been gathered, the text and commentaries consulted and the doctrine checked, they have never been distilled and integrated into a coherent whole. These sermons remind me of a baker who puts out all the ingredients for a cake on the kitchen work surface, but does not leave time to mix them together, let alone cook them in the oven. It has potential, but is indigestible in its present form. Some sermons are like Ephraim (Hos. 7:8), 'a flat loaf', half-baked at best!

The priority of preaching

Preaching is the most public, the most visible and potentially the most effective aspect of ministry. It therefore deserves to be given serious attention. Relegating it to the AOB of our busy ministries will not do. We must raise it up the agenda and give it the time it deserves.

The most important advice usually given in this regard, quite rightly, is that we need to immerse ourselves in the text we are to preach.[6] This means we must unhurriedly listen to the text, studying it in depth, unravelling its problems, clarifying its meaning, placing it in context and letting it address us first. To begin with, our concentration must be on the text itself, but once we have prayerfully worked through it and begun truly to know it, we will certainly want to turn to other aids such as commentaries.

Some argue that we should only consult the commentaries late in the day, if at all. I do not believe, however, that we should leave it too late. Good commentaries written with preachers in mind, which rules out a lot, can help us

---

6. The word 'immerse' comes from Michael Quicke, who uses the analogy of swimming as a metaphor for preaching in *360 Degree Preaching, Hearing, Speaking and Living the Word* (Grand Rapids: Baker Academic, 2003), pp. 130, 140–152. Other writers make the same point either using different metaphors or in direct terms. Paul Scott Wilson, in *The Four Pages of the Sermon: A Guide to Biblical Preaching* (Nashville: Abingdon Press, 1999), sets out a complete week's timetable.

unlock the text and see things in it that, unaided, we might miss. Reading a commentary is certainly no substitute for our personal engagement with the text, but ignoring them smacks to me of arrogance, as if we are self-sufficient and do not need the wisdom of others to assist us. At the very least they can help us sort out the historical context or the geographic movements in many texts of which, unless we are graduates in Ancient Near East history, we are probably ignorant. In reality, they are conversation partners that can teach us much more than a few necessary 'facts'. They are tools to assist us in our work. They should never become straitjackets that lock us in and restrain us from speaking a word from God, or interfering busybodies that interpose themselves between us and the text itself when they are not welcome. Preaching demands more than immersing ourselves in the text, but we do not need to do less than this and must give ourselves time to do it.

Once we have done that, we have only just begun our journey to the sermon. Our sermon needs a 'big idea': that is, a coherent thread that runs through it all.[7] As Haddon Robinson has imaginatively expressed it, 'A sermon should be a bullet not buckshot.'[8] It needs structure; it needs clothing with illustration and interest; it needs application;

---

7. See Keith Willhite and Scott M. Gibson (eds.), *The Big Idea of Biblical Preaching: Connecting the Bible to People* (Grand Rapids: Baker Books, 1998).

8. Haddon Robinson, *Biblical Preaching: The Development and Delivery of Expository Messages* (Grand Rapids: Baker Books, 1993), p. 33.

it needs a good conclusion and ending – all matters which any standard book on preaching explain. But if we have not immersed ourselves in the text, the rest will struggle to swim and not sink!

In recent days, much has been made of the need to reimagine the text for the contemporary context. 'Imagination' has become a buzzword. Thomas Long has pointed out how contemporary hermeneutics has become a 'true friend of the preacher', 'precisely at the juncture between human imagination and textual interpretation'.[9] It is true that our work on the text could leave us with some interesting reflections which seem to have little meaning for today. Imagination overcomes this. But imagination needs discipline, sermons that lift off need anchoring, and interpretation needs a text to interpret. Imagination too easily becomes a flight of fancy. Commitment to the priority of scripture arises from a doctrinal conviction in God's written word as a living word and God's preached word as an eventful word. Therefore the one must connect closely with the other.

Many preachers live hand to mouth and therefore set scant fare before their congregations. Many intend to set aside time to prepare, but somehow other things take over. They are like cooks who are always intending to cook

---

9. Thomas Long, 'The Use of Scripture in Contemporary Preaching', in David Day, Jeff Astley and Leslie J. Francis (eds.), *A Reader on Preaching* (Aldershot: Ashgate, 2005), p. 37. Originally published in *Interpretation* 44 (1990), pp. 341–352.

a decent meal, but end up more times than they would like to admit popping into the local takeaway instead. Preachers who want to set a nutritious diet before their congregation will resist the pressures of busyness and start preparation early. They will ensure that regular investments of study occur so that their homiletic capital both grows and is constantly refreshed. To change the imagery once more, the good preacher draws on a reservoir, which needs to be continually refilled. If the inflow is inadequate, the reservoir not only runs dry but also runs the risk of becoming stagnant, and the sermon soon smells!

The reality is that preachers need not just to be working on next Sunday's sermon, but reading elsewhere in scripture and reading other things (or studying selectively on the Internet) which will contribute to stimulating their minds as well as providing illustrations and provoking applications. John Wesley once wrote to one of his travelling preachers in typically forthright terms,

What has exceedingly hurt you in time past, nay, and I fear, to this day, is want of reading. I scarce ever knew a preacher read so little. And perhaps, by neglecting it, have lost the taste for it. Hence your talent in preaching does not increase. It is just the same as it was seven years ago. It is lively, but not deep; there is little variety; there is no compass of thought. Reading only can supply this, with meditation and daily prayer . . . O begin! Fix some part of every day for private exercise. You may acquire the taste which you have not: what is tedious at first, will afterward be pleasant. Whether you like it or no, read and pray daily. It is for your life; there is no other way; *else you will be a trifler all your days, and a pretty, superficial preacher.* Do justice to your own soul; give it time and means to grow; do not starve yourself any longer. Take up your cross and be a Christian altogether. Then will all the children of God rejoice (not grieve) over you.[10]

Wesley could have been addressing many today. His strictures are right on target in a day when we are confronted with lively but not deep preaching, in which there is no 'compass of thought'.

The only way to overcome the problem is to confront the idol of busyness and unmask it, revealing it to be the impotent idol that it is, just as surely as Elijah confronted Baal on Mount Carmel.[11] Busyness may be popular, but so was Baal. And Baal could never light the fire!

Preacher, keep yourself from idols.

---

10. Cited by Mel Lawrenz in *The Dynamics of Spiritual Formation* (Baker Books, 2000), p. 61f., italics mine.
11. 1 Kgs 18:16–46.

12. THE IDOL OF FAMILIARITY

Our final idol is a subspecies of the idol of professionalism. It is the idol that appears in the preacher's home without anyone being aware of its arrival. Satan smuggles it in while we are not paying attention. It is the idol of familiarity. We become so accustomed to holy things, so used to handling them, so comfortable around the word of God, that we cease to wonder at it. Cutting the corners in our own spiritual discipline, we begin to take it for granted and, as in a marriage, when that happens the spark goes out and the flame of passion dies.

I am interested in the impact this idol has. It may have one of three different effects on us, leading to triviality, or cynicism, or hype, depending on our personality.

Triviality

Triviality is probably the most common response this idol

draws from us. Because preachers handle God's word regularly, we are in constant danger of reducing its awesome message to something trivial. The Palace of Westminster, which houses the House of Commons and House of Lords and so much else, is an awesome building. Its physical grandeur, its sumptuous decoration, its imposing management, its frequent reminders of significant moments in the history of the nation, all point to the power of the decisions taken there. When I was being shown around on one occasion I asked my MP whether he ever took it for granted. He replied, 'It's easy to do so when you work here daily, so every now and again I attach myself to a tour and listen to the guide explaining its history, its architecture and its business, so I don't forget.' Many preachers need to attach themselves, as it were, to a tour guide, since they seem to have forgotten the awesome nature of their message.

Familiarity can mean that the wonder of scripture is reduced, its truth trivialized, its demands cheapened, its radicalism domesticated, its significance rendered inconsequential, its mystery tamed, its delivery made banal. The gospel has become a petty, trifling thing that merely confirms our comfortable way of life or helps us to make some psychological adjustment to ease our path just a trifle more.

Principal Rainey commended A. J. Gossip, when he was a student, for choosing a great subject and preaching on it. It is the right thing to do even though you cannot always do it. Gossip later commented that it was 'very sound advice, though it is not the easy path'. He admitted, 'So long as we are pirouetting with some petty bit of text on the outskirts of things, we feel easy in our minds.'[1] Fred Craddock wisely pointed out that 'small topics are like pennies; even when polished to a high gloss, they are still pennies'.[2] Conversely, he advised, 'It is almost impossible for a sermon on a matter of major importance to the listeners to be totally uninteresting and without impact.'[3]

I have heard sermons on Genesis 1 that make it sound as if its intention was to be a draft of a recycling leaflet produced by the local council. David and Jonathan are no more than examples of friendship. The feeding of the five thousand becomes a lesson in sharing scarce resources. Luke 15 has been turned into a good parenting guide. And Colossians 3:15 is about how we have discovered God's will when we feel psychological peace about our decisions. Divine revelation is often diluted until it becomes nothing more than a version of Samuel Smiles's *Self-Help* manual.

Walter Brueggemann chose to introduce his Lyman Beecher lectures at Yale University in 1989 at just this point.

> The gospel is thus a truth widely held, but a truth greatly reduced. It is a truth that has been flattened, trivialized,

1. Quoted in William Barclay, *Testament of Faith* (London and Oxford: Mowbrays, 1975), p. 73.
2. Fred. B. Craddock, *Preaching* (Nashville: Abingdon, 1985), p. 49.
3. ibid.

and rendered inane. Partly, the gospel is an old habit among us, neither valued nor questioned. But more than that, our technical way of thinking reduces mystery to problem, transforms assurance to certitude, revises quality to quantity, and so takes the categories of biblical faith and represents them in manageable shapes.[4]

Brueggemann's answer is that we need to be 'poets that speak against a prose world'.[5] The prophets, he says, were poets who took the word in all its 'resilient power'[6] and delivered it in fresh and lively ways. 'If the text', he argues, 'is to claim authority it will require neither the close reasoning of a canon lawyer, nor the precisions of a technician, but it will require an artist to render the text in quite fresh ways, so that the text breaks life open among the baptized as it never has before.'[7]

This answer to the problem certainly has merit. Warren Wiersbe lends support to it in saying, 'In our noble attempt to be biblical preachers, we have so emphasised the analytical that we've forgotten the poetic. We see the trees waving their branches, but we hold the branches still,

---

4. Walter Brueggemann, *Finally Comes the Poet: Daring Speech for Proclamation* (Minneapolis: Fortress, 1989), pp. 1–2.

5. ibid., p. 3. Brooks's contrary comments are interesting in this connection, in Phillips Brooks, *Lectures on Preaching*, delivered at Yale Divinity School, 1877 (London: Allenson and Co., n.d.), pp. 109–110.

6. Brueggemann, *Finally Comes the Poet*, p. 10.

7. ibid., p. 9.

examine them scientifically, leaf and twig, and all the while fail to hear the trees clapping their hands at the glory of God.'[8]

We should exercise a little caution, however, since it has to be said that not all can be poets, as the prophets were, and not all of scripture is made up of poetry. The conversations of Jesus in John's Gospel and the discussion of theology in Romans, for example, seem to contain a fair degree of close reasoning. Moreover, not everyone understands poetry or enjoys it.

My own answer is somewhat different. It is simply to say we should constantly ask whether what we preach matters or not in the light of eternity. The greatest questions about our preaching are: Does it matter? Have we said anything which is of eternal significance? So what? Or have we simply filled the air with pretty little phrases and thoughts that trip off the tongue, but might be said by a thousand other communicators who have no distinctive gospel message to offer a dying world?

Not even oratory can make up for a lack of substance. When commenting on Barack Obama's speech-making, Philip Collins wrote, 'In fact, no speech will work if it is genuinely trite.'[9] Too much preaching does not work because it is trite.

---

8. Warren Wiersbie, *Preaching and Teaching with Imagination* (Grand Rapids: Baker Books, 1994), pp. 35–36.

9. *The Times*, 6 November 2008, p. 20.

Cynicism

Another way of handling our familiarity with God's truth is cynicism. Cynicism, remember, originated with Cynic philosophy which had an important part to play in rhetorical training. The Cynics perfected the art of using sarcasm and ridicule to move audiences, of believing the worst about people or about the way things were done, and of saying so. They delighted in undermining the accepted standards and conventions of their day.

Few preachers would express cynicism from the pulpit (except maybe about those whose religious practice is different from theirs!) since in many nice middle-class congregations it is likely to prove unacceptable. Cynicism is often expressed behind closed doors, often brought about by being worn down in ministry or disappointed by others, even if people are 'professional' enough to maintain their public guard.

Cynicism is deeply antithetical to love. It prevents 1 Corinthians 13 from becoming a reality in our Christian communities. It leads us to dishonour others, keep records of wrongs, delight in others' downfalls, undermine others, mistrust them and despair of the hope that anyone will ever improve or anything will ever be achieved. In being cynical we not only fail to measure up to Paul's ideal, but we demonstrate that we do not believe Jesus, who taught that much of the work of the kingdom is hidden,[10] and that we do not trust the power of the Spirit to be an effective agent of change.[11]

Maturity demands that we keep a healthy balance between idealism and reality. We should never let defeatism swallow up our idealism and reduce us to cynicism. Equally, we should never let idealism be out of sympathy with realism. Cynicism is like bindweed in a garden. If we do not combat it radically, it will soon creep into everything, including our preaching, strangling everything that is alive. It will be impossible to control. Our guard will slip even in the pulpit and our true feelings will be let out. When that happens, our preaching will be devoid of the first prerequisite of persuasion, that of authenticity. People will know we do not really believe the gospel we preach. We will have become the 'resounding gong' or 'clanging cymbal' of 1 Corinthians 13:1.

Hype

Another way of battling against familiarity is the very opposite of trivialization. It is that of hype. If trivialization understates the gospel, hype overstates it.

Struggling to convey the wonder of the gospel, desiring to combat its routine familiarity and longing to witness its transforming effect on the congregation, some preachers

---

10. Matt. 13:24–52.
11. 2 Cor. 3:18; Phil. 2:13.

go in for hyping up their message. It may get the congregation excited, but . . .

The worst example I ever heard was a well-known
preacher on the international circuit who said in my
hearing, 'God does not know how to work naturally. He
only ever works supernaturally.' His audience whooped
and clapped at the thought. I believe that God can and
does work supernaturally, but such a claim, however well
intended, is heretical. It rubbishes the doctrines of creation
and incarnation. It leads to an otherworldly discipleship
which encourages escapism and is contrary to the biblical
teaching on holiness. The audience may have loved it, but
they deserved to be taught better.

Hype comes in various forms.

- Sometimes it is hype in condemning the sins of
  others, forgetting that we are all fallen creatures and
  'but for grace of God we are liable to fall too'.[12] It is,
  in British terms, a *Daily Mail* style of preaching
  where the headlines always adopt inflated language
  and scream at people. Wrongdoers are always
  monsters, evil and perverts. Victims are always
  'exceptional'. No-one and nothing is ever average
  or ordinary.
- Sometimes it is hype about a coming revival, a
  spiritual breakthrough that is just around the corner,

12. See Gal. 6:1.

on which evangelicalism has alternately thrived and
been cast down in despondency.

- Sometimes it is inflated claims about the gospel. 'Come
  to Jesus' and all your problems will instantly disappear.
  There will never be 'a shadow' in life, nor 'a cloud in the
  sky' for the one who trusts and obeys.[13] Try telling that
  to David on the run, Jeremiah in the pit, Daniel in the
  lions' den or Jesus in the garden of Gethsemane.

- Sometimes we promise an experience of the Spirit or
  even make some general pastoral comment that
  promises a trouble-free Christian life that we cannot
  deliver in practice.

- Sometimes our hype consists of driving our
  congregations and making unreasonable demands on
  them that takes no account of the realities of their
  demanding lives. 'The true disciple must . . . the true
  disciple will . . . '

- Sometimes we over-egg the conditions required for
  God's blessing. 'God will only bless us if . . . ' We
  forget that he is a merciful God who remembers we
  are made of dust. We forget that he knows all about
  the complex creatures we are and the muddled
  brokenness of our lives and graciously chooses to
  work in and through us nonetheless.

---

13. The hymn 'Trust and Obey' by John Henry Sammis (1846–1919)
    contains the lines, 'Not a shadow can rise, not a cloud in the skies,
    but his smile quickly drives it away; not a doubt, nor a fear, not a
    sigh, nor a tear, can abide when we trust and obey.'

These may all be worthy attempts to break through the mundane and the monotony of Christian discipleship in a fallen world and to lift yet-to-be-fully-redeemed individuals to a higher level of Christian experience. The intention is laudable, but the method invites trouble rather than solving the problem. We should never preach from the safety of the pulpit what we cannot sustain in the intimacy of the pastoral conversation.

Phillips Brooks described this type of preaching as a boiler that has no connection with an engine. Plenty of steam escapes, but it is never converted into energy that proves productive.[14] It makes a lot of noise, but it fails to produce any movement. Brooks's dictum, as we have mentioned, was: 'The sermon must never set a standard which it is not really meant that man should try to realize in life.'[15]

The perils of familiarity are not new. The book of Leviticus spends a good deal of time addressing the issue. Overfamiliarity may have contributed to the death of Aaron's sons, Nadab and Abihu, as they offered 'unauthorized fire' to the Lord.[16] The subject is also addressed in Leviticus 22, where various instructions are given to priests to help them avoid its pitfalls. In several case studies the chapter warns of the occupational hazards of the priesthood.

---

14. Brooks, *Lectures*, p. 44.
15. ibid., p. 142.
16. Lev. 10.

Case 1: Service may become inadmissible (vv. 1–9) when we see ourselves as a special case. We have no special immunity from the normal spiritual disciplines, in fact, more is required of us.

Case 2: Familiarity may become negligence (vv. 10–16) when we erode boundaries and become presumptuous before God. We dare not treat the things of God casually.

Case 3: Offerings may become unacceptable (vv. 17–33), however well intended, if they are blemished.[17]

What was true of the Aaronic priesthood is equally true for today's preachers. Standards must never be eroded, advantage of our intimacy with God never taken, nor obedience lessened.

From the false idols of ministry that seek our allegiance and devotion – the idols of professionalism, busyness and familiarity – may God protect us, that we might serve only him who alone is the one, true, living God.

Preacher, keep yourself from idols.

---

17. For a fuller exposition along these lines, see Derek Tidball, *The Message of Leviticus: Free to be Holy*, BST (Nottingham: IVP, 2005), pp. 266–268.

EPILOGUE

Every preacher longs to be met with the response Paul received when he preached the gospel in Thessalonica. They treated his words 'not as a human word, but as it actually is, the word of God' (1 Thess. 2:13) and consequently 'turned to God from idols to serve the living and true God' (1 Thess. 1:9). Perhaps their rejection of idolatry was connected to the preacher himself being free from idolatry and modelling wholehearted service to the living God (1 Thess. 2:1–12). As a Jew, Paul was of course a monotheist and not given to idol worship. Yet Jews recognized that not all idols were carved in wood and covered in paint. They viewed 'greed', or 'evil desires', as idolatry (Col. 3:5) because it made what had been created the object of worship instead of the Creator.

Preachers are very unlikely to bow down in worship to hand-carved idols of stone, but they are very vulnerable to serving idols of a more subtle kind. This book has reviewed some of the idols which any preacher will encounter, but not all. To my list, you may add yours. Furthermore, it must be remembered that idolatry is only one kind of temptation which preachers encounter. There are others, such as envy and pride, which are only alluded to in the foregoing pages. The pulpit is indeed simultaneously the most privileged and the most perilous place to stand.

The antidote to idolatry is nothing less than submission to the living God, in whose exclusive service we are.

To ensure this, two great hymns of the faith should be the regular prayer of every preacher. With Frances Ridley Havergal we should pray:

> Take my voice and let me sing;
> Always, only, for my King:
> Take my lips, and let them be
> Filled with messages from thee.[1]

And with Charles Wesley we should pray:

> Jesus, confirm my heart's desire
> To work and speak and think for thee;
> Still let me guard the holy fire,
> And still stir up thy gift in me.[2]

---

1. From 'Take My Life, And Let It Be'.
2. From 'O Thou Who Camest From Above'.

INDEX OF SCRIPTURE REFERENCES

For more details of books published by IVP, visit our website where you will find all the latest information, including:

Book extracts   Downloads
Author interviews   Online bookshop
Reviews   Christian bookshop finder

You can also sign up for our regular email newsletters, which are tailored to your particular interests, and tell others what you think about this book by posting a review.

We publish a wide range of books on various subjects including:

Christian living   Small-group resources
Key reference works   Topical issues
Bible commentary series Theological studies